Knitted Finger Puppets

Knitted Finger Puppets

Susie Johns

For my children Josh, Lillie and Edith, who are not too old to play with finger puppets and who are a constant support and inspiration.

First published 2012 by
Guild of Master Craftsman Publications Ltd
Castle Place, 166 High Street, Lewes,
East Sussex, BN7 1XU

Reprinted 2013

ISBN 978-1-86108-814-7

The publishers and author can accept no legal
responsibility for any consequences arising from
the application of information, advice or instructions
given in this publication.

A catalogue record for this book is available
from the British Library.

Publisher: Jonathan Bailey
Production Manager: Jim Bulley
Managing Editor: Gerrie Purcell
Senior Project Editor: Virginia Brehaut
Managing Art Editor: Gilda Pacitti
Design: Ali Walper
Pattern Checker: Anni Howard

Set in Gill Sans

Colour origination by GMC Reprographics
Printed and bound in China

Why we love finger puppets

PLAY-ACTING AND STORYTELLING ARE AN essential part of any child's development and these quirky little finger puppets can help to inspire some wonderfully creative play. With 30 assorted characters inhabiting five different make-believe scenarios, you and your child can use the puppets to interpret favourite tales, songs and rhymes, or make up your own stories and scripts.

The projects are made from four-ply yarn using small needles to allow for as much detail as possible. Being small, they are relatively quick to knit – though don't underestimate the time needed for making up and sewing in yarn ends. They are not only an outlet for your creativity but also a great way to use up oddments of yarn. Best of all, they are fun to make.

You don't need much knitting experience: just the ability to follow a pattern and the patience and dexterity to stitch small pieces of knitting together. Why not start with something simple, such as the Monkey or the Robot? Even the more complex designs such as the Scarecrow are not really more difficult: they just have more component parts.

Making these finger puppets isn't just about knitting the pieces: it is about constructing them and giving each of them a personality. An aptitude for making three-dimensional items is something that I developed through making papier mâché models for the children's magazine *Art Attack* for 12 years, and also for my own three children. I hope you enjoy making these knitted characters as much as I enjoyed designing them.

Contents

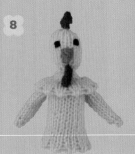

17

18

19

20

21

22

23

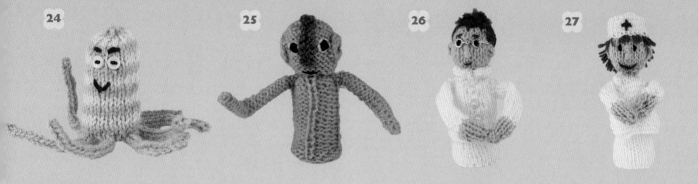

At the circus

He flies through the air with the greatest of ease...but this
agile little gymnast can also stand on his head, somersault, bounce
a ball or do whatever you want him to do.

Tony trapeze

Materials

4-ply knitting yarn in pale peach (A), black (B),
  turquoise (C) and red (D)
Pair of 2.75mm (UK12:US2) knitting needles
Tapestry needle
Polyester toy filling

Size

Tony's body measures approximately 2½in (6.25cm) in length.

Tension

See page 142

Body and head (made in one piece)

Using 2.75mm needles and A, cast on 22 sts.

Row 1: K each st tbl.

Row 2: P to end.

Rows 3–5: K to end.

Row 6: P to end.

Row 7: Join in B; K2B, 8A, 2B, 8A, 2B.

Row 8: P2B, 8A, 2B, 8A, 2B.

Row 9: K3B, 6A, 4B, 6A, 3B.

Row 10: P4B, 4A, 6B, 4A, 4B.

Row 11: K5B, 2A, 8B, 2A, 5B; cut A.

Row 12: Using B p to end.

Row 13: K to end.

Row 14: P to end; do not cut B but join in C.

Row 15: Using C, k to end.

Row 16: P to end.

Continue in stocking stitch for 10 rows, changing colour after every two rows; rejoin A.

Row 27: K9C, 4A, 9C.

Row 28: K8C, 6A, 8C; cut C.

Row 29: Using B, (k5, k2tog), using A, (k2tog, k4, k2tog), using B, (k2tog, k5) (18 sts).

Row 30: Using B, (k3, k2tog), k8A, using B, (k2tog, k3) (16 sts); cut B.

Row 31: Using A, k to end.

Row 32: P to end.

Row 33: K6, (incl in next st) 4 times, k6 (20 sts).

Beg with a p row, work 5 rows in stocking stitch; cut A; rejoin B.

Beg with a k row and using B, work 4 rows in stocking stitch.

Row 43: (k2tog) 10 times (10 sts).

Row 44: P to end.

Cut yarn and thread through all sts.

Arms (make 2)

Using 2.75mm needles and A, cast on 4 sts.

Row 1: Incl in each st (8 sts).

Beg with a p row, work 9 rows in stocking stitch; cut A and join in B.

Using B, work a further 2 rows in stocking stitch; do not cut B but join in C.

Using C, work a further 2 rows in stocking stitch; cut C.

Using B, k 1 row, then cast off purlwise.

Making up

On cast-on edge of body, fold first few rows to wrong side and stitch in place to create a hem. Join back seam using backstitch on wrong side; turn right sides out and, using yarn A, stitch a running stitch around neckline. Insert a small amount of stuffing into head then pull up yarn to close gap and fasten off. Stitch underarm seams; do not cut off yarn ends but use them to stuff arms. Stitch arms to top of body at either side. Using B, embroider eyes; embroider a mouth using D. Using A, embroider a nose in satin stitch and ears in bullion stitch. (See pages 152–3 for more details about embroidering facial features.)

Is she a fearsome wild animal or someone dressed up in a cute tiger suit? You decide. Either way, Tamsin is one of the most popular and well-loved performers the circus ring has ever seen.

Tamsin tiger

Materials

4-ply knitting yarn in ivory (A), tangerine (B), geranium red (C) and buttercup yellow (D) plus small amounts of peppermint and black

Pair of 2.75mm (UK12:US2) knitting needles

Pair of 2.25mm (UK13:US1) knitting needles

4 x 2.25mm (UK13:US1) double-pointed knitting needles

Wire or plastic narrow bangle for hoop

Tapestry needle

Polyester toy stuffing

Button or circle of plastic 1¾in (4.5cm) in diameter for plinth

Size

Tamsin's body measures approximately 2½in (6.25cm) in length.

Tension

See page 142

Body and head (made in one piece)

Using 2.75mm needles and A, cast on 20 sts.

Row 1: K each st tbl.

Row 2: P to end.

Row 3: K to end.

Rows 4–6: P to end.

Beg with a k row, work 2 rows in stocking stitch.

Do not break off A. Join in B. Cont in stocking stitch, working (2 rows in B, then 4 rows in A) 3 times. Break off B.

Row 27: K4, (k2tog) twice, k4, (k2tog) twice, k4 (16 sts).

Beg with a p row, work 3 rows in stocking stitch.

Row 31: K3, (inc in next st, k2) 3 times, inc in next st, k3 (20 sts).

Row 32: P to end.

Row 33: K2, (inc in next st, k2) 6 times (26 sts).

Beg with a p row, work 9 rows in stocking stitch.

Row 43: K2, (k2tog, k2) 6 times (20 sts).

Row 44: P to end.

Row 45: (K2tog) 10 times.

Break off yarn and thread through rem 10 sts.

Paws and front legs (make 2)

Using 2.75mm needles and A, cast on 6 sts.

Row 1: Inc in each st (12 sts).

Row 2: P to end.

Row 3: (K2tog) 6 times (6 sts).

Row 4: P to end.

Do not break off A. Join in B.

Cont in stocking stitch, working (2 rows in B, then 2 rows in A) twice. Cast off.

Tail

Using 2.75mm needles and A, cast on 6 sts.

Row 1: Knit.

Row 2: Purl; do not break off A. Join in B. Cont in stocking stitch, working in 2-row stripes until you have completed the 5th stripe in B, then work two further rows in B.
Cast off.

Ears (make 2)

Using 2.75mm needles and B, cast on 5 sts.

Row 1: K each st tbl.

Row 2: P to end.

Row 3: K to end.

Row 4: P to end.

Row 5: K2tog, k1, k2tog (3 sts).

Row 6: P to end.

Row 7: K3tog.

Break off yarn and fasten off.

Collar

Using 2.25mm needles and C, cast on 14 sts.

Row 1: K each st tbl.
Cast off knitwise.

Making up the tiger

At base of body, fold first few rows to wrong side along purl ridge and stitch in place to create a hem. Stitch back seam of body and head. Run a length of yarn through the stitches at neckline, stuff head and draw up yarn to close opening and shape neck. Stitch seams on paws and front legs and attach each one to body. Stitch ears to either side of head. Wrap collar around neck and stitch in place.

Join side edges of tail with a neat mattress-stitch seam, pulling up the seam slightly to cause the tail to curve, then stitch base of tail to centre back, just above hem. Embroider the face. Using peppermint yarn, stitch three horizontal stitches for each eye, then with black yarn, stitch a small vertical stitch across the centre stitch of each eye and a horizontal stitch above each eye. Embroider a nose in satin stitch and use straight stitches to form mouth. Using B, stitch whiskers and stripes at top of head.

Hoop

Using 2.25mm needles and C, cast on 60 sts.
Row 1: K each st tbl.
Row 2: P to end.
Row 3: K to end.
Row 4: P to end.
Cast off, leaving a tail of yarn.

Making up the hoop

Stitch the two short ends together then wrap the knitted piece around the bangle and oversew edges together neatly.

Plinth

This little item, shaped like a drum, is an important prop in any circus ring. It can be used by any members of the troupe when they are performing their tricks.

Using set of four 2.25mm double-pointed needles and D, cast on 6 sts and divide stitches equally over three needles.
Round 1: Inc1 in each st (12 sts).
Round 2: K to end.
Round 3: Inc1 in each st (24 sts).
Round 4: K to end.
Round 5: (K1, inc1) 12 times (36 sts); cut B and join in C.
Round 6: Using C, k to end of round. Purl 2 rounds; cut C and rejoin D. Using B, knit 8 rounds; cut D and rejoin C.
Round 17: Using C, k to end of round. Purl 2 rounds; cut C and rejoin D.
Round 20: Using D, k to end of round.
Round 21: (K1, k2tog) 12 times (24 sts).
Round 22: K to end.
After completing round 22, insert a large button or circle cut from plastic, to create a flat top for the plinth.
Round 23: (K2tog) 12 times (12 sts).
Round 24: K to end.
Round 25: (K2tog) 6 times; cut yarn and thread through rem 6 sts.

Making up the plinth

Before closing up the hole in the base, stuff well with polyester filling.

Using C and a long stitch, embroider zigzag pattern around side of plinth.

Ball

This two-colour ball is a useful prop that can be used by any of the circus performers.

Using set of four 2.25mm double-pointed needles and D, cast on 6 sts and divide stitches equally over three needles.
Round 1: Inc1 in each st (12 sts).
Round 2: K to end of round.
Round 3: (Inc1, k1) 6 times (18 sts). Knit 4 rounds, then cut D and join in C. Using C, knit 4 rounds.
Round 12: (K2tog, k1) 6 times (12 sts).
Round 13: K to end of round.
Round 14: (K2tog) 6 times. Cut yarn and thread through rem 6 sts.

Making up the ball

Add stuffing through gap, then pull yarn end to close up hole.

Guaranteed to raise a smile and a laugh, this mischievous little monkey will delight circus audiences with his truly amazing acrobatic antics and tricks.

Malachi monkey

Materials

4-ply knitting yarn in buff (A), beige (B) and geranium red (C), plus small amounts of black and dark red
Pair of 2.75mm (UK12:US2) knitting needles
Pair of 2.25mm (UK13:US1) knitting needles
2 × 2.75mm (UK12:US2) double-pointed knitting needles
2 × 2.25mm (UK13:US1) double-pointed knitting needles
Tapestry needle
Polyester toy stuffing

Size

Malachi's body measures approximately 2½in (6.25cm) in length.

Tension

See page 142

Body and head

Using 2.75mm needles and A, cast on 20 sts.

Row 1: K each st tbl.

Row 2: P to end.

Row 3: K to end.

Rows 4–6: P to end.

Beg with a k row, work 20 rows in stocking stitch.

Row 27: K4, (k2tog) twice, k4, (k2tog) twice, k4 (16 sts).

Beg with a p row, work 3 rows in stocking stitch.

Row 31: K3, (inc1, k2) 3 times, inc1, k3 (20 sts).

Row 32: P to end.

Row 33: K2, (inc1, k2) 6 times (26 sts).

Beg with a p row, work 9 rows in stocking stitch.

Row 43: K2, (k2tog, k2) 6 times (20 sts).

Row 44: P to end.

Row 45: (k2tog) 10 times (10 sts).

Row 46: (P2tog) 5 times.

Cut yarn and thread through rem 5 sts.

Paws and arms (make 2)

Using two 2.75mm double-pointed needles and A, cast on 3 sts.

Row 1: Inc1 in each st (6 sts).

Row 2: P to end.

Row 3: (K1, inc1) 3 times (9 sts).

Row 4: P to end.

Row 5: (K1, k2tog) 3 times (6 sts).

Row 6: P to end.

Row 7: (K1, k2tog) twice (4 sts);

do not turn but, with RS facing, *slide sts to other end of needle and k4; rep from * 12 times more. Cast off.

Ears (make 2)

Using 2.75mm knitting needles and A, cast on 5 sts.

Row 1: K each st tbl.

Row 2: P to end.

Row 3: K to end.

Row 4: P to end.

Row 5: K2tog, k1, k2tog (3 sts).

Row 6: P to end.

Row 7: K to end.

Row 8: P3tog; cut yarn and fasten off.

Face

Using 2.25mm needles and B, cast on 3 sts.

Row 1: P to end.

Row 2: Inc1 in each st (6 sts).

Row 3: P to end.

Row 4: Inc1 in each st (12 sts).

Row 5: P to end.

Row 6: (K1, inc1) 6 times (18 sts).

Row 7: P to end.

Row 8: K to end. Cast off.

Tail

Using two 2.25mm double-pointed needles and A, cast on 3 sts.

Row 1: K3; do not turn but, with RS facing, *slide sts to other end of needle and k3, rep from * 18 times more. Cast off.

Fez

Using a set of four 2.25mm double-pointed knitting needles and C, cast on 18 sts and divide between three needles.

Round 1: K each st tbl.

Knit 7 rounds.

Round 9: (K1, k2tog) 6 times (12 sts).

Round 10: (K2tog) 6 times (6 sts).

Round 11: (K2tog) 3 times; cut yarn and thread through rem 3 sts.

Making up

Stitch hem and back seam then stuff the head. Stitch seams on first few rows of paws and attach each one to body. Stitch ears to either side of head. Stitch tail to lower edge of back. Join seam on face piece and stitch to front of head, tucking yarn ends inside. Stitch hat to top of head, adding a little stuffing if you wish.

Embroider the face: with beige yarn, stitching three vertical stitches for each eye and then a horizontal stitch for the eyebrows. Then, with black yarn stitch a small horizontal stitch across the centre stitch of each eye and another across the top of the eye, and a small horizontal stitch for the nose. Using dark red, stitch a single straight stitch to form the mouth, couching it in place using two or three small, discreet stitches. (See pages 152–3 for more details about embroidering facial features.)

Overseeing the circus entertainment is an important job and Russell, with his smart red tail coat, bow tie, top hat and dapper moustache, is ready to crack his whip and keep everything under control.

Russell ringmaster

Materials

4-ply knitting yarn in black (A), pale grey (B), turquoise (C), white (D), beige (E), geranium red (F) and chocolate (G)

Black embroidery thread

1 small red button

Button or circle of plastic approximately 1in (2.5cm) in diameter

Pair of 2.75mm (UK12:US2) knitting needles

2 x 2.75mm (UK12:US2) double-pointed knitting needles

4 x 2.25mm (UK13:US1) double-pointed knitting needles

Tapestry needle

Plastic drinking straw

Size

Russell's body measures approximately 2½in (6.25cm) in length.

Tension

See page 142

Trousers

Using two 2.75mm double-pointed needles and A, cast on 10 sts; do not cut A but slide sts to other end of needle and join in B.

Row 1: Using B, k to end; do not cut B but turn work and pick up A.

Row 2: Using A, p to end; do not cut A but slide sts to other end of needle and pick up B.

Row 3: Using B, p to end; turn.

Continue in this way, working single rows in alternate colours until 35 rows have been worked, ending with a row in B.

Cast off using A.

Cut B; using A, and with RS facing, pick up and k24 sts along one long edge of work.

Knit 2 rows and cast off knitwise; cut yarn and fasten off.

Cummerbund, torso and head

Cummerbund

On opposite edge of trousers, using 2.75mm needles and C, and with RS facing, pick up and k24 sts.

Knit 3 rows, cut yarn.

Torso and head

Using D, beg with a k row, work 8 rows in stocking stitch.

Row 12: K1, k2tog, (k2, k2tog) 5 times, k1 (18 sts).

Row 13: P to end; cut yarn and join in E.

Row 14: Using E, k to end.

Row 15: P to end.

Row 16: K1, inc1, (k2, inc1) 5 times, k1 (24 sts).

Beg with a p row, work 11 rows in stocking stitch.

Row 28: (K2tog) 12 times (12 sts).

Row 29: (P2tog) 6 times.

Cut yarn and thread through rem 6 sts.

Arms (make 2)

Using 2.75mm needles and E, cast on 4 sts.

Row 1: K to end.

Row 2: P to end.

Row 3: Inc1 in each st (8 sts).

Row 4: P to end.

Row 5: K to end.

Row 6: P to end; cut E and join in D.

Rows 7–9: Using D, k to end.

Beg with a p row, work 19 rows in stocking stitch. Cast off.

Jacket

Main part

Using 2.75mm needles and F, cast on 28 sts.

Row 1 (WS): K each st tbl.

Row 2: K to end.

Row 3: K1, p to last st, k1.

Rep rows 2 and 3 eight times more.

Row 20: K4, [(k2tog) twice, k4] 3 times (22 sts).

Row 21: P to end.

Row 22: (K2tog) 11 times (11 sts).

Row 23: P to end.

Cast off.

Sleeves (make 2)

Using 2.75mm needles and F, cast on 11 sts.

Row 1 (WS): K each st tbl.

Row 2: K to end.

Beg with a p row, work 11 rows in stocking stitch.

Row 14: K1, sl1, k1, psso, k5, k2tog, k1 (9 sts).

Row 15: P to end.

Row 16: K1, sl1, k1, psso, k3, k2tog, k1 (7 sts).

Row 17: P to end.

Cast off.

Hat

Using 2.25mm needles and A, cast on 1 st and k into front, back and front of this st (3 sts).

Row 1: Inc1 in each st (6 sts).

Row 2: P to end.
Row 3: Inc1 in each st (12 sts).
Row 4: P to end.
Row 5: Inc1 in each st (24 sts).
Beg with a p row, work 11 rows in stocking stitch.
Row 17: (K1, inc1) 12 times (36 sts).
Row 18: P to end.
Row 19: (K2, inc1) 12 times (48 sts).
Row 20: P to end.
Cast off.

Bow tie

Using 2.25mm needles and A, cast on 11 sts.
Row 1: K each st tbl.
Row 2: P to end.
Row 3: K to end.
Cast off knitwise.

Whip

Using 2.25mm needles and G, cast on 28 sts.
Row 1: K each st tbl.
Knit 2 rows.
Cast off.

Making up

Stitch back seam of trousers, torso and head. Run a length of yarn through the stitches at neckline, stuff head and draw up yarn to close opening and shape neck. Wrap jacket around body, placing the two side edges at centre front. Stitch edges together about ½in (1cm) down from cast-off edge and stitch button on top of this join. Fold back edges above this point and stitch in place to form lapels.

Stitch arm seams, stuffing with any remaining yarn ends, then fold over approximately ½in (1cm) at top of each one, to create extra bulk; attach to top of main piece of jacket at shoulders. Stitch sleeve seams, slip each one over one of the arms and stitch to jacket.

Using yarn E, make ears from bullion stitch and oversew the central line of stitches to form a nose. Use black embroidery thread to embroider eyes, eyebrows, a moustache and small mouth. (See pages 152–3 for more

details about embroidering facial features.) Stitch the seam on the hat, place button in top of hat and stuff, then stitch the hat to top of the head.

To make the bow tie, fold under ¼in (3mm) on each short edge then bind tail of yarn two or three times around centre to form a bow shape. Stitch to front of neck. To make up the whip, cut a 3in (7.5cm) length from a narrow plastic drinking straw, wrap the strip of knitting around it and oversew cast-on and cast-off edges together. Tuck in end, leaving one yarn end dangling. Fold one of the ringmaster's hands over the whip handle and stitch in place.

No circus can be complete without a clown to entertain
the crowds and this one, with his bright costume, funny hat
and big red nose, fits the bill perfectly.

Capability clown

Materials

4-ply knitting yarn in geranium red (A), banana (B),
   Prussian blue (C), white (D), pale peach (E), tangerine (F),
   turquoise (G), ivory (H), plus small amount of black
2 small white buttons
Pair of 2.75mm (UK12:US2) knitting needles
Pair of 2.25mm (UK13:US1) knitting needles
4 × 2.25mm (UK13:US1) double-pointed knitting needles
Tapestry needle
Polyester toy filling

Size

Capability's body measures approximately
3in (7.5cm) in length.

Tension

See page 142

Trousers

Using 2.75mm needles and A, cast on 12 sts.

Row 1: K each st tbl.

Row 2: P to end; do not cut A but join in B.

Row 3: Using B, k to end.

Row 4: P to end.

Row 5: Using A, k to end.

Row 6: P to end.

Rep rows 3 to 6 eight times more; cast off and cut B.

Hem

Using 2.75mm needles and A, with RS of trousers facing, pick up and k22 sts, evenly spaced, along one long edge.

Row 1: P to end.

Cast off knitwise.

Belt

Using 2.75mm needles and C, with RS of trousers facing, pick up and k20 sts along opposite long edge.

Beg with a p row, work 6 rows in stocking stitch.

Cast off purlwise.

Torso and head

Using 2.75mm needles and B, cast on 20 sts.

Beg with a k row, work 12 rows in stocking stitch.

Row 13: K4, (k2tog) twice, k4, (k2tog) twice, k4 (16 sts).

Row 14: P to end; cut B and join in D.

Row 15: Using D, k4, (inc1 in next st) twice, k4, (inc1 in next st) twice, k4 (20 sts).

Beg with a p row, work 9 rows in stocking stitch.

Row 25: K1, (k2tog, k2) 4 times, k2tog, k1 (15 sts).

Row 26: (P1, p2tog) 5 times (10 sts).

Row 27: (K2tog) 5 times; cut yarn and thread through rem 5 sts.

Arms (make 2)

Using 2.75mm needles and E, cast on 4 sts.

Row 1: Inc1 in each st (8 sts).

Row 2: P to end.

Beg with a p row, work 3 rows in stocking stitch; cut E and join in A.

Using A, work 2 rows in stocking stitch;

cut A and join in B.

Using B, work 10 rows in stocking stitch.

Cast off.

Braces (make 2)

Using 2.25mm needles and F, cast on 25 sts.

Row 1: K each st tbl.

Row 2: P to end.

Row 3: K to end.

Cast off knitwise.

Hat (in two pieces)

Crown

Using 2.25mm needles and G, cast on 1 st and k into front, back, front, back and front of this st (5 sts).

Row 1: Inc1 in each st (10 sts).

Row 2: P to end.

Row 3: (K1, inc1) 5 times (15 sts).

Row 4: P to end.

Row 5: (K2, inc1) 5 times (20 sts).

Row 6: P to end.

Row 7: (K3, inc1) 5 times (25 sts).

Row 8: P to end.

Row 9: K to end.

Cast off knitwise.

Brim

Using 2.25mm needles and G, cast on 5 sts.

Knit 68 rows.

Cast off.

Ruff

Using 2.25mm needles and H, *cast on 6 sts using cable method, cast off 3 sts; rep from * 9 times more (30 sts); turn.
Row 1: K to end.
Cast off all sts and cut yarn, leaving a long tail.
Thread the tail of yarn in and out of sts on cast-off edge.

Nose

Using 2.25mm needles and A, cast on 6 sts.
Beg with a k row, work 8 rows in stocking stitch.
Cast off.

Making up the clown

Fold belt over and stitch cast-off edge to top of trousers then, with right sides together, stitch up the back seam using backstitch then turn right sides out. Stitch back seam of torso and head in the same way. Run a length of yarn through the stitches at neckline, stuff head and draw up yarn to close opening and shape neck.

Stitch arm seams, stuffing with any remaining yarn ends, then attach to body at shoulders. Stitch trousers to bottom edge of torso. Stitch one end of each of the braces to the back of the belt, cross the two pieces over at centre back and stitch to belt at front.

Stitch buttons to ends of braces. Place ruff over head and pull up yarn end to fit neck, then secure with a few stitches.

Using one of the yarn ends on the nose, stitch a running stitch all round edge and pull up tight. With purl stitches as RS, stuff the nose with a tiny wisp of polyester filling or with a scrap of yarn, then stitch to centre of face. Use yarn A, embroider mouth, and make ears using bullion stitch, then use a little black yarn to embroider eyes and eyebrows. (See pages 152–3 for more details about embroidering facial features.)

Stitch seam on crown of hat and stitch to top of head, then stitch two short ends of hat brim together, run a gathering stitch around one long edge and pull up to fit head; stitch in place around bottom edge of crown.

Ring mat (made in one piece)

This colourful ring mat matches the plinth on page 19 and provides an ideal performance area for all the circus folk.

Using set of four 2.25mm double-pointed needles and B, cast on 6 sts and divide equally between over needles.
Round 1: Inc1 in each st (12 sts).
Round 2 and each even-numbered round: K to end of round.

Round 3: (Inc1, k1) 6 times (18 sts).
Round 5: (Inc1, k2) 6 times (24 sts).
Round 7: (Inc1, k3) 6 times (30 sts)
Round 9: (Inc1, k4) 6 times (36 sts).
Round 11: (Inc1, k5) 6 times (42 sts).
Round 13: (Inc1, k6) 6 times (48 sts).
Round 15: (Inc1, k7) 6 times (54 sts).
Round 17: (Inc1, k8) 6 times (60 sts).
Round 19: (Inc1, k9) 6 times (66 sts); cut B and join in A.
Round 20: Using A, k to end.
Round 21: (Inc1, k10) 6 times (72 sts).
Round 23: (Inc1, k11) 6 times (78 sts).
Cast off.

Making up the ring mat

Weave in yarn ends on WS of work; press under a damp cloth.

Whether she is deftly walking a tightrope,
dancing around the ring or selling ice-creams in the interval,
Bella always adds a touch of glamour to the big top.

Bella ballerina

Materials

4-ply knitting yarn in beige (A), raspberry (B), tangerine (C),
  pink (D) and papaya (E), plus a small amount of black
Pair of 2.75mm (UK12:US2) knitting needles
4 x 2.75mm (UK12:US2) double-pointed knitting needles
Pair of 2.25mm (UK13:US1) knitting needles
Tapestry needle
A few pink glass seed beads (optional)
Polyester toy stuffing

Size

Bella's body measures approximately 2½in (6.25cm)
in length.

Tension

See page 142

Body and head (made in one piece)

Using 2.75mm needles and A, cast on 20 sts.

Row 1: K each st tbl.

Row 2: P to end.

Row 3: K to end.

Rows 4–6: P to end.

Beg with a k row, work 20 rows in stocking stitch.

Row 27: K1, (k2tog, k2) 4 times, k2tog, k1 (15 sts).

Row 28: P to end.

Row 29: K1, k2tog, k2, k2tog, k1, k2tog, k2, k2tog, k1 (11 sts).

Row 30: P to end.

Row 31: K to end.

Row 32: P to end.

Row 33: K3, inc1, k1, inc2 (by knitting into front, back and front of next st), k1, inc1, k3 (15 sts).

Row 34: P to end.

Row 35: K5, inc2, k1, inc1, k1, inc2, k5 (20 sts).

Beg with a p row, work 9 rows in stocking stitch.

Row 45: (K2tog) 10 times (10 sts).

Row 46: P to end.

Row 47: (K2tog) 5 times.

Cut yarn and thread through rem 5 sts.

Arms (make 2)

Using 2.75mm needles and A, cast on 4 sts.

Row 1: Inc1 in each st (8 sts).

Beg with a p row, work 17 rows in stocking stitch. Cast off.

Dress

Using set of four 2.75mm double-pointed needles and B, cast on 21 sts and divide equally over three needles.

Round 1: K each st tbl.

Knit 6 rounds.

Round 8: (K2, inc1) 7 times (28 sts).

Knit 11 rounds; cut yarn and join in C.

Cast-off round: Inc1 in first st of round, pass first st on right-hand needle over second st, * inc1 in next st, pass first and second sts on right-hand needle over first st, rep from * until all sts have been cast off; cut yarn and fasten off.

Peplum skirt

Using set of four 2.75mm double-pointed needles and B, cast on 22 sts and divide equally over three needles.

Round 1: K each st tbl.

Round 2: (K1, inc1) 11 times (33 sts).

Round 3: (K2, inc1) 11 times (44 sts).

Knit 5 rounds; cut yarn and join in D.

Cast-off round: Inc1 in first st of round, pass first st on right-hand needle over second st, * inc1 in next st, pass first and second sts on right-hand needle over first st, rep from * until all sts are cast off; cut yarn and fasten off.

Hairband

Using 2.25mm knitting needles and B, cast on 30 sts.

Cast off.

Flower

Using 2.25mm knitting needles and D, cast on 8 sts, cut yarn, leaving a tail. Thread this on to a tapestry needle, then take this through each st in turn, starting with the first st of the row, forming a ring. Draw up, not too tightly, to form a rosette with the stitch loops forming petals.

Bun

Using 2.25mm knitting needles and E, cast on 4 sts.

Beg with a k row, work 20 rows in stocking stitch.

Row 21: (K2tog) twice (2 sts).

Beg with a p row, work 13 rows in stocking stitch.

Cast off.

Making up

At base of body, fold first few rows to wrong side along purl ridge and stitch in place to create a hem. Stitch back seam of body and head. Run a length of yarn through the stitches at neckline, stuff head and draw up yarn to close opening and shape neck. Stitch arm seams and attach to top of body at shoulders. Slip dress on to body and stitch top edge of bodice to body, just below arms. Slip peplum skirt over dress and stitch cast-on edge to waistline.

Use yarn E to stitch hair in satin stitch, taking stitches all along base of hairline to crown of head, then, starting from the wider end of the strip, roll up the bun and stitch to top of head; add a few extra lengths of yarn to create a fringe, securing them at the front of the bun, and trim ends fairly short for a spiky 'punk rock' effect. Wrap headband around head and stitch ends together, then stitch flower to one side, adding a few small beads to the centre if you wish, stitching these in place with matching sewing thread.

Use yarn A to embroider a nose in satin stitch and ears in bullion stitch, adding a small bead earring to each one, if you wish. Use a little raspberry yarn to embroider a mouth, using a single Swiss darning stitch and black yarn for eyes. (See pages 152–3 for more details about embroidering facial features.)

To make a pair of bracelets and a choker, simply wrap two strands of raspberry yarn around wrists and neck.

In the farmyard

This smiling scarecrow looks too cheerful to frighten the birds, but when it comes to storytelling and play-acting he will be a welcome participant in any farmyard tale.

Spud scarecrow

Materials

4-ply knitting yarn in chocolate (A), mustard (B), olive green (C) and geranium red (D), plus a small amount of buttercup yellow and black
1 small brown button
Pair of 2.75mm (UK12:US2) knitting needles
Pair of 2.25mm (UK13:US1) knitting needles
Tapestry needle
Polyester toy stuffing
Plastic drinking straw

Size

Spud's body measures approximately 2½in (6.25cm) in length.

Tension

See page 142

Body and head
(made in one piece)

Using 2.75mm needles and A, cast on 24 sts.

Row 1: K to end.

Row 2: P to end.

Rows 3–4: K to end.

Row 5: (K1, p1) 12 times.

Rep the last row 25 times more.

Row 31: (K2, k2tog) 6 times (18 sts); cut A and join in B.

Row 32: Using B, p to end.

Row 33: K to end.

Row 34: P to end.

Row 35: K6, (incl in next st) 6 times, k6 (24 sts).

Beg with a p row, work 11 rows in stocking stitch.

Row 47: (K2tog) 12 times (12 sts).

Row 48: (P2tog) 6 times; cut yarn and thread through rem 6 sts.

Twig arms

Using 2.25mm needles and A, cast on 22 sts.

Row 1: K each st tbl.

Knit 2 rows.

Cast off.

Jacket

Main part

Using 2.75mm needles and C, cast on 30 sts.

Knit 2 rows.

Row 3: K to end.

Row 4: P to end.

Rep rows 3 and 4 eight times more.

Row 21: K5, [(k2tog) twice, k4] 3 times, k1 (24 sts).

Row 22: K to end.

Row 23: (K2tog) 12 times (12 sts).

Row 24: P to end.

Cast off knitwise.

Sleeves (make 2)

Using 2.75mm needles and C, cast on 10 sts.

Knit 3 rows.

Beg with a p row, work 17 rows in stocking stitch.

Cast off.

Collar

Using 2.75mm needles and C, cast on 12 sts.

Row 1: K to end.

Row 2: Incl in first st, k10, incl in last st (14 sts).

Cast off.

Hat

Using 2.75mm needles and A, cast on 6 sts.

Row 1: Incl in each st (12 sts).

Row 2: K to end.

Row 3: Incl in each st (24 sts).

Knit 11 rows.

Row 15: (K1, incl) 12 times (36 sts).

Row 16: K to end.

Row 17: (K2, incl) 12 times (48 sts).

Row 18: K to end.

Cast off knitwise.

Scarf

Using 2.25mm needles and D, cast on 36 sts, then cast off.

Flower

Using 2.25mm needles and D, cast on 8 sts, cut yarn, leaving a tail. Thread this on to a tapestry needle then take through each st in turn, starting with the first st of the row, forming a ring. Draw up, not too tightly, to form a rosette with the stitch loops forming petals.

Making up

Stitch back seam of body and head. Run a length of yarn through the stitches at neckline, stuff head and draw up yarn to close opening and shape neck. Fold first few rows of body along ridge on row 4 to outside and stitch in place.

Wrap jacket around body, placing the two side edges at centre front. Stitch edges together about ½in (1cm) down from cast-off edge and stitch button on top of this join. Fold back edges above this point and stitch in place to form lapels, then stitch cast-on edge of collar in place on top edge of jacket, around back of neck, and stitch collar points to front of jacket, above lapels. To make pocket flaps, pick up and k4 sts on one side of jacket, using yarn C, then cast off; do the same on the other side.

To make up the twig arms, cut two 2in (5cm) lengths from a narrow plastic drinking straw, wrap a strip of knitting around each one and oversew cast-on and cast-off edges together. Attach to top of main piece of jacket at shoulders. Make two bundles of short lengths of buttercup-yellow yarn and stitch around ends of arms. Trim ends of yarn. Stitch sleeve seams, slip one over each of the arms and stitch to jacket at shoulders.

Stitch the seam on the hat and then the hat to the top of the head. Stitch flower to side of hat. Using buttercup-yellow yarn, make a centre to the flower using satin stitch. Using C, embroider leaf at either side of the flower using a lazy daisy stitch.

Use black yarn to embroider eyes in satin stitch, and a smiling mouth by stitching a line of running stitches, then a row of vertical stitches along this line. Knot scarf around neck.

Practise your clucks and squawks: here comes the
cheeky little hen known as 'Rietta', strutting around the farmyard,
pecking at niblets of corn and the occasional tasty worm.

Henrietta hen

Materials

4-ply knitting yarn in banana yellow (A), tangerine (B) and
   geranium red (C), plus a small amount of black
Pair of 2.75mm (UK12:US2) knitting needles
Pair of 2.25mm (UK13:US1) knitting needles
Tapestry needle
Polyester toy stuffing

Size

Henrietta's body measures approximately 2in (5cm) in length.

Tension

See page 142

Body

Using 2.75mm needles and A, cast on 20 sts.

Row 1: K each st tbl.
Row 2: P to end.
Row 3: K to end.
Row 4: P to end.
Row 5: K1, (yfwd, k2tog) 9 times, k1.
Beg with a p row, work 19 rows in stocking stitch.
Row 25: (K3, k2tog) 4 times (16 sts).
Row 26: (P2, p2tog) 4 times (12 sts).
Row 27: (K1, k2tog) 4 times (8 sts).
Row 28: (P2, p2tog) twice.
Cut yarn and thread through rem 6 sts.

Head

Using 2.75mm needles and A, cast on 24 sts.

Row 1: K each st tbl.
Row 2: P to end.
Row 3: K to end.
Row 4: P to end.
Row 5: K1, (yfwd, k2tog) 11 times, k1.
Beg with a p row, work 5 rows in stocking stitch.
Row 11: K1, (k2tog, k2) 5 times, k2tog, k1 (18 sts).
Row 12: P to end.
Row 13: (K1, k2tog) 6 times (12 sts).
Row 14: (P2tog) 6 times (6 sts).
Row 15: (Inc1) 6 times (12 sts).
Row 16: P to end.
Row 17: K1, (inc1, k2) 3 times, inc1, k1 (16 sts).

Beg with a p row, work 10 rows in stocking stitch.
Row 28: (P2tog) 8 times (8 sts).
Row 29: (K2tog) 4 times.
Cut yarn and thread through rem 4 sts.

Wings (make 2)

Using 2.75mm needles and A, cast on 1 st.

Row 1: Inc2 (k into front, back and front of st) (3 sts).
Row 2: P to end.
Row 3: K1, inc2, k1 (5 sts).
Row 4: P to end.
Row 5: (K1, inc1) twice, k1 (7 sts).
Row 6: P to end.
Row 7: K1, inc1, k3, inc1, k1 (9 sts).
Beg with a p row, work 10 rows in stocking stitch.
Row 18: (P2tog) twice, p1, (p2tog) twice; cut yarn and thread through rem 5 sts.

Beak

Using 2.75mm needles and B, cast on 6 sts.

Row 1: K each st tbl.
Row 2: P to end.
Row 3: (K2tog) 3 times (3 sts).
Row 4: P3tog; fasten off.

Wattle

Using 2.75mm needles and C, cast on 9 sts.
Cast off.

Comb

Using 2.25mm needles and C, (cast on 4 sts, cast off 3 sts, return st on RH needle to LH needle) 3 times (3 sts).
Row 1: Knit each st tbl.
Cast off.

Making up

Stitch back seam of body. Do the same with the head. Use yarn ends to neaten the wing tips, then fold each wing in half (but do not stitch edges together) and attach wings to body, with cast-off edges at either side of base of neck. Stuff head with polyester filling, then place on top of body and wings, and stitch firmly in place.

Fold beak in half and stitch sides together to form a tight cone, then attach to centre front of head. Fold wattle in half and oversew edges, then stitch in place below beak. Stitch comb to top of head. Embroider eyes using black yarn.

Young Millie, the farmer's daughter, is a big help to everyone around the farmyard, doing all kinds of chores and looking pretty as a picture in her blue dress, petticoat and apron.

Millie milkmaid

Materials

4-ply knitting yarn in white (A), pale peach (B) and sky blue (C), plus small amounts of buttercup yellow and geranium red

Black embroidery thread (optional)

Pair of 2.75mm (UK12:US2) knitting needles

Tapestry needle

Polyester toy stuffing

Size

Millie's body measures approximately 2½in (6.25cm) in length.

Tension

See page 142

Body and head
(made in one piece)

Using 2.75mm needles and A, cast on 20 sts.

Row 1: K each st tbl.
Row 2: P to end.
Row 3: K to end.
Row 4: P to end.
Row 5: K1, (yfwd, k2tog) 9 times, k1.
Beg with a p row, work 13 rows in stocking stitch; cut A and join in B. Using B, work a further 10 rows in stocking stitch.
Row 29: K4, [(k2tog) twice, k4] twice (16 sts).
Row 30: P to end.
Row 31: K to end.
Row 32: P to end.
Row 33: K6, (incl in next st) 4 times, k6 (20 sts).
Beg with a p row, work 5 rows in stocking stitch.

Row 39: K9, (incl in next st) twice, k9 (22 sts).
Row 40: P to end.
Row 41: K to end.
Row 42: P to end.
Row 43: K9, sl1, k1, psso, k2tog, k9 (20 sts).
Row 44: P to end.
Row 45: (K2tog) 10 times (10 sts).
Row 46: (P2tog) 5 times; cut yarn and thread through rem 5 sts.

Dress

Using 2.75mm needles and C, cast on 40 sts.

Row 1: K each st tbl.
Row 2: K to end.
Row 3: P to end.
Rep rows 2 and 3 four times more.
Row 12: (K2tog) 20 times (20 sts).
Beg with a p row, work 4 rows in stocking stitch.
Row 17: P7, k6, p7.
Row 18: K7, p6, k7.
Row 19: P7, k2, cast off 2 sts knitwise, k2 including st on needle after cast-off, p7.
Row 20: (K2tog) 4 times, k1, turn and cast off purlwise.
Rejoin yarn to rem 9 sts, then k1, (k2tog) 4 times; turn and cast off purlwise.

Arms and sleeves
(make 2)

Using 2.75mm needles and B, cast on 4 sts.

Row 1: Incl in each st (8 sts).
Beg with a p row, work 9 rows in stocking stitch; cut B and join in C.
Row 11: K to end.
Row 12: P to end.
Row 13: Incl in each st (16 sts).
Beg with a p row, work 5 rows in stocking stitch.
Row 19: (K2tog) 8 times (8 sts).
Cast off purlwise.

Apron

Using 2.75mm needles and A, cast on 80 sts. Cast off.
Identify the centre 8 sts on the cast-on edge, pick up and k these sts, then knit 8 rows and cast off.

Making up

At base of body, fold first few rows to wrong side along eyelet row and stitch in place to create a picot hem. Stitch back seam of body and head. Run a length of yarn through the stitches at neckline, stuff head and draw up yarn to close opening and shape neck.

Stitch back seam of dress, slip on to body and stitch top of bodice to neckline. Thread a length of yarn C in and out of stitches on decrease

row at waistline and pull up to gather slightly. Stitch seams on each arm and sleeve piece, adding a little stuffing to the sleeves if you wish. Stitch tops of sleeves to sides of bodice. Tie apron around waist.

Cut 12 × 16in (15cm) lengths of yellow yarn, tie around centre with another length of yarn and stitch to centre top of head. Plait ends and tie each one with a length of sky-blue yarn. Stitch another bundle of short strands of yarn to head, to form a fringe. At the back of the head, embroider straight stitches from the nape of the neck to the top of the head, to complete the hairstyle.

Use black embroidery thread or black yarn to embroider eyes and eyebrows, and geranium-red yarn for mouth. Using yarn B, embroider nose in satin stitch. (See pages 152–3 for more details about embroidering facial features.)

Every farmyard needs a pig to eat up the food scraps.
This little pink piggy has a body constructed in two layers
with padding in between to give her a plump shape.

Polly pig

Materials

4-ply knitting yarn in pink (A)

Small amount of black yarn

Pair of 2.75mm (UK12:US2) knitting needles

Tapestry needle

Polyester toy stuffing

Size

Polly's body measures approximately 2½in (6.25cm)
in length.

Tension

See page 142

Body and head (made in one piece)

Using 2.75mm needles and A, cast on 5 sts.

Row 1: Inc1 in each st (10 sts).

Row 2: P to end.

Row 3: Inc1 in each st (20 sts).

Beg with a p row, work 24 rows in stocking stitch.

Row 28: K to end.

Row 29: K2, (inc1 in next st, k4) 3 times, inc1, k2 (24 sts).

Row 30: P to end.

Row 31: K2, inc1, k5, inc1, k6, inc1, k5, inc1, k2 (28 sts).

Row 32: P to end.

Row 33: K2, inc1, k6, inc1, k8, inc1, k6, inc1, k2 (32 sts).

Beg with a p row, work 21 rows in stocking stitch.

Row 55: (K2tog, k2) 4 times, (k2, k2tog) 4 times (24 sts).

Row 56: P to end.

Row 57: (K2tog) 12 times (12 sts).

Row 58: P to end.

Row 59: Inc1 in each st (24 sts).

Beg with a p row, work 9 rows in stocking stitch.

Row 69: (K2tog) 12 times (12 sts).

Row 70: P to end.

Row 71: (K2tog) 6 times.

Cut yarn and thread through rem 6 sts.

Trotters (make 2)

Using 2.75mm needles and A, cast on 4 sts.

Row 1: Inc1 in each st (8 sts).

Beg with a p row, work 7 rows in stocking stitch.

Cast off.

Ears (make 2)

Using 2.75mm knitting needles and A, cast on 1 st.

Row 1: Inc1 (2 sts).

Row 2: P to end.

Row 3: Inc1 in each st (4 sts).

Row 4: P to end.

Row 5: Inc1, k2, inc1 (6 sts).

Beg with a p row, work 5 rows in stocking stitch.

Cast off.

Snout

Using 2.75mm needles and A, cast on 16 sts.

Row 1: K each st tbl.

Row 2: P to end.

Rows 3–5: K to end.

Row 6: P to end.

Row 7: K to end.

Cast off knitwise.

Tail

Using 2.75mm knitting needles and A, cast on 25 sts.

Cast-off row: K1,* k2tog, slip first st on RH needle over 2nd st, rep from * until 1 st remains; fasten off.

Making up

With right sides together, stitch the sides with a neat backstitch seam, leaving a gap near base of body close to the garter-stitch ridge. Turn right sides out and, inserting stuffing into gap in seam, stuff head and the space between the inner and outer body parts. Stitch the seam closed using mattress stitch on the right side of work. Sew a running stitch around neckline and pull up to tighten slightly, then attach the top of the inner part of the body to the neck with a few discreet stitches.

To form the snout, fold the knitted piece in half along the garter-stitch ridge, right sides out, and roll up tightly, holding it in place with a few stitches, then stitch to front of head. Fold the tail, oversewing the long edges together tightly and leaving about ¼in (3mm) at one end unstitched. Stitch this flat end to centre back, just above hem.

Fold each trotter in half lengthways and stitch, then attach to sides of body, about ¾in (1.5cm) below neckline. Stitch ears in place at each side of head. Use black yarn to embroider eyes and nostrils.

With his chunky jumper and flat cap, Fred's ready to tackle any job
on the farm, whether it's ploughing a field, shearing a sheep
or picking green apples to put in his basket.

Farmer Fred

Materials

4-ply knitting yarn in mustard (A), chocolate (B), ivory (C),
  pale peach (D), buff (E) and apple green (F), plus a small
  amount of grey and black
Pair of 2.75mm (UK12:US2) knitting needles
Pair of 2.25mm (UK13:US1) knitting needles
2 x 2.25mm (UK13:US1) double-pointed knitting needles
Tapestry needle
Polyester toy stuffing

Size

Fred's body measures approximately 2½in (6.25cm)
in length.

Tension

See page 142

Body and sweater (in one piece)

Using 2.75mm needles and A, cast on 24 sts.

Row 1: K to end.

Row 2: P to end.

Rows 3–4: K to end.

Row 5: (K1, p1) 12 times.

Rep row 5 11 times more; cut yarn and join in B.

Rows 17–18: Using B, k to end; cut yarn and join in C.

Beg with a k row, work 10 rows in stocking stitch.

Row 29: K2, (k2tog, k4) 3 times, k2tog, k2 (20 sts).

Row 30: P to end.

Row 31: (K2, k2tog) 5 times (15 sts).

Change to 2.25mm needles.

Row 32: (K1, p1) 7 times, k1.

Row 33: (P1, k1) 7 times, p1.

Work 6 rows more in rib as set.

Cast off in rib.

Head

Using 2.75mm needles and D, cast on 10 sts.

Row 1: P to end.

Row 2: Inc1 knitwise in each st (20 sts).

Beg with a p row, work 11 rows in stocking stitch.

Row 14: (K2tog) 10 times (10 sts).

Row 15: (P2 tog) 5 times.

Cast off knitwise.

Arms (make 2)

Using 2.75mm knitting needles and D, cast on 4 sts.

Row 1: K to end.

Row 2: P to end.

Row 3: Inc1 in each st (8 sts).

Beg with a p row, work 21 rows in stocking stitch.

Cast off.

Sleeves (make 2)

Using 2.25mm needles and C, cast on 9 sts.

Row 1: (K1, p1) 4 times, k1.

Row 2: (P1, k1) 4 times, p1.

Rep rows 1 and 2 three times more.

Change to size 2.75mm needles and, beg with a k row, work 10 rows in stocking stitch.

Row 19: K1, sl1, k1, psso, k3, k2tog, k1 (7 sts).

Row 20: P to end.

Row 21: K1, sl1, k1, psso, k1, k2tog, k1 (5 sts).

Row 22: P to end.

Cast off.

Cap

Using 2.25mm knitting needles and E, cast on 1 st and k into front, back, front, back and front of this st (5 sts).

Row 1: Inc1 in each st (10 sts).

Row 2: P to end.

Row 3: (K1, inc1) 5 times (15 sts).

Row 4: P to end.

Row 5: (K2, inc1) 5 times (20 sts).

Row 6: P to end.

Row 7: (K3, inc1) 5 times (25 sts).

Row 8: P to end.

Row 9: K to end.

Cast off knitwise.

Making up

Stitch back seam of body and sweater. Fold first few rows to inside and stitch in place to form a hem. On head, run a length of yarn through the stitches at cast-on edge, stuff head and draw up

yarn to close opening and shape neck. Fold over top of sweater, push head inside this opening and stitch firmly to inside edge.

Stitch arm seams, stuffing with any remaining yarn ends, then fold over approximately ½in (1cm) at top of each one, to create extra bulk; attach to top of sweater at shoulders. Stitch sleeve seams and turn back cuffs, slip each sleeve over one of the arms and stitch to sweater.

Using yarn D, make ears from detached buttonhole stitch and oversew the central line of stitches to form a nose. Use black yarn to embroider eyes and mouth and grey to embroider eyebrows, each of which is a single small stitch. (See pages 152–3 for more details about embroidering facial features.) For hair, embroider lines of satin stitch in grey starting in front of one ear and working round to the other ear.

Having purl side as right side of hat, stitch back seam, then stitch hat to head, using a few stitches to shape a small peak at the front.

Basket of fruit

This could be a basket of green apples, or you could use red if you prefer. The basket can be made for other characters and scenarios, too: perhaps the pirate crew would like a basket of oranges or lemons to help prevent scurvy, or Mrs Moppet (page 137) might like an empty basket in which to collect laundry?

Basket

Using 2.75mm needles and E, cast on 3 sts.
Row 1: Inc1 in each st (6 sts).
Row 2: P to end.
Row 3: Inc1 in each st (12 sts).
Row 4: P to end.
Row 5: (K1, inc1) 6 times (18 sts).
Row 6: P to end.
Row 7: (K1, inc1) 9 times (27 sts).
Row 8: K to end.
Beg with a k row, work 20 rows in stocking stitch.
Cast off.

Handles (make 2)

Using two 2.25mm double-pointed needles and E, cast on 2 sts.
Row 1: K2; do not turn but slide sts to other end of needle.
Rep row 1 19 times more.
Cast off.

Apples (make 7)

Using 2.25mm knitting needles and F, cast on 3 sts.
Row 1: Inc1, k1, inc1 (5 sts).
Row 2: P to end.

Row 3: Inc1, k3, inc1 (7 sts).
Row 4: P to end.
Row 5: K to end.
Row 6: P to end.
Row 7: K2tog, k3, k2tog (5 sts).
Row 8: P to end.
Row 9: K2tog, k1, k2tog (3 sts).
Cast off.

Making up the basket

Stitch seam on basket. Roll a few rows over to right side along top edge and secure with a few discreet stitches. To make each apple, thread tail of yarn in tapestry needle and stitch a running stitch all round edge of knitted fabric, place a tiny piece of wadding in the centre and pull up yarn to gather; secure with a few stitches.

Stuff basket half-full with toy stuffing, then add a layer of spare strands of yarn E. Stitch the apples together in a neat cluster and place on top of basket. Stitch in place, taking needle through sides of basket and right through the apples.

Dennis is a friendly duck. He is happy to swim around the duckpond or snooze in the shade of a haystack, and he is always ready and willing to take part in your storytelling.

Dennis duck

Materials

4-ply knitting yarn in white (A) and tangerine (B),
   plus a small amount of black
Pair of 2.75mm (UK12:US2) knitting needles
2 × double-pointed 2.75mm (UK12:US2) knitting needles
Tapestry needle
Polyester toy stuffing
Short length of plastic drinking straw

Size

Dennis's body measures approximately 2¼in (5.5cm) in length

Tension

See page 142

Body and head (in one piece)

Using 2.75mm needles and A, cast on 20 sts.

Row 1: K each st tbl.
Row 2: P to end.
Row 3: K to end.
Row 4: P to end.
Row 5: P to end.
Beg with a p row, work 19 rows in stocking stitch.
Row 25: (K3, k2tog) 4 times (16 sts).
Row 26: (P2, p2tog) 4 times (12 sts).
Row 27: (K1, k2tog) 4 times (8 sts).
Row 28: (P2, p2tog) twice (6 sts).
Beg with a k row, work 6 rows in stocking stitch for neck.
Row 35: (Inc1) 6 times (12 sts).
Row 36: P to end.
Row 37: (K1, inc1) 6 times (18 sts).
Beg with a p row, work 5 rows in stocking stitch.
Row 43: (K1, k2tog) 6 times (12 sts).
Row 44: P to end.
Row 45: (K2tog) 6 times (6 sts).
Row 46: (P2 tog) 3 times; cut yarn and thread through rem 3 sts.

Wings (make 2)

Using 2.75mm needles and A, cast on 1 st.

Row 1: Inc2 (k into front, back and front of st) (3 sts).
Row 2: P to end.
Row 3: K1, inc2, k1 (5 sts).
Row 4: P to end.
Row 5: (K1, inc1) twice, k1 (7 sts).
Row 6: P to end.
Row 7: K1, inc1, k3, inc1, k1 (9 sts).
Beg with a p row, work 10 rows in stocking stitch.
Row 18: (P2tog) twice, p1, (p2tog) twice; cut yarn and thread through rem 5 sts.

Beak

Using 2.75mm needles and B, cast on 1 st.

Row 1: Inc2 (3 sts).
Row 2: P to end.
Row 3: K1, inc2, k1 (5 sts).
Beg with a p row, work 4 rows in stocking stitch.
Row 8: P2tog, p1, p2tog (3 sts).
Row 9: K to end.
Row 10: P to end.
Row 11: K1, inc2, k1 (5 sts).
Beg with a p row, work 5 rows in stocking stitch.
Cast off.

Making up

Stitch back seam of body and head. Stuff head with polyester filling, then insert a short length of plastic drinking straw into neck. Stitch a few discreet stitches across base of neck to hold the straw in place.

Attach wings to body, at either side of base of neck. Use yarn ends to neaten the wing tip. Fold beak in half at narrowest point and stitch sides together by oversewing, then attach to centre front of head.

Make a small bundle of yarn A and stitch to top of head, then trim to form a short tuft. Embroider eyes using black yarn.

Fairyland fun

In her pretty pink dress and golden crown, this beautiful princess
can help you to act out all kinds of favourite fairy stories
– and there is sure to be a happy ending.

Princess Clarissa

Materials

4-ply knitting yarn in white (A), pale peach (B), pink (C),
   buttercup yellow (D) and gold (E), plus small amount
   of blue
Embroidery thread in black
1 fancy button
Pair of 2.75mm (UK12:US2) knitting needles
Pair of 2.25mm (UK13:US1) knitting needles
Tapestry needle
Polyester toy stuffing

Size

Princess Clarissa's body measures approximately 2½in
(6.25cm) in length.

Tension

See page 142

Body and head
(made in one piece)

Using 2.75mm needles and A, cast on 20 sts.

Row 1: K each st tbl.

Row 2: P to end.

Row 3: K to end.

Row 4: P to end.

Row 5: K1, (yfwd, k2tog) 9 times, k1.

Beg with a p row, work 23 rows in stocking stitch.

Row 29: K4, [(k2tog) twice, k4] twice (16 sts).

Row 30: P to end; cut A and join in B.

Row 31: Using B, k to end.

Row 32: P to end.

Row 33: K6, (inc1 in next st) 4 times, k6 (20 sts).

Beg with a p row, work 5 rows in stocking stitch.

Row 39: K9, (inc1 in next st) twice, k9 (22 sts).

Row 40: P to end.

Row 41: K9, sl1, k1, psso, k2tog, k9 (20 sts).

Beg with a p row, work 3 rows in stocking stitch.

Row 45: (K2tog) 10 times (10 sts).

Row 46: (P2tog) 5 times (5 sts); cut yarn and thread through rem 5 sts.

Skirt

Using 2.75mm needles and C, cast on 40 sts.

Row 1: K each st tbl.

Row 2: P to end.

Row 3: K to end.

Row 4: P to end.

Row 5: K1, (yfwd, k2tog) 19 times, k1.

Row 6: P to end.

Row 7: K to end; do not cut C but join in D.

Row 8: (P1D, 1C) to end of row; cut yarn D.

Beg with a k row, work 10 rows in stocking stitch.

Row 19: (K2tog) 20 times (20 sts).

Row 20: P to end.

Row 21: K to end.

Cast off knitwise.

Arms and sleeves
(make 2)

Using 2.75mm needles and B, cast on 4 sts.

Row 1: Inc1 in each st (8 sts).

Beg with a p row, work 3 rows in stocking stitch; cut B and join in A.

Using A, work 2 rows in stocking stitch; cut A and join in C.

Using C, work 6 rows in stocking stitch.

Row 13: Inc1 in each st (16 sts).

Beg with a p row, work 3 rows in stocking stitch.

Row 17: (K2tog) 8 times (8 sts).

Cast off purlwise.

Collar

Using 2.75mm needles and C, cast on 40 sts.

Row 1: K each st tbl.

Row 2: P to end.

Cast off knitwise.

Crown

Using 2.25mm needles and E, cast on 22 sts.

Row 1: K each st tbl.

Rows 2–3: K to end.

Cast off knitwise.

Belt

Using 2.25mm needles and E, cast on 24 sts.

Cast off, knitting each st tbl.

Making up

At base of body, fold first few rows to wrong side along eyelet row and stitch in place to create a picot hem. Stitch back seam of body and head. Run a length of yarn through the stitches at neckline, stuff head and draw up yarn to close opening and shape neck.

At the base of the skirt, fold first few rows to wrong side along eyelet row and stitch in place to create a picot hem. Stitch back seam of skirt; run a length of yarn through the stitches at waistline, slip on to body and stitch top of skirt to body at waistline, pulling up yarn to tighten top of skirt slightly. Stitch belt just below top of skirt, joining the ends at the back.

Stitch seams on each arm and sleeve piece, adding a little stuffing to them if you wish, and stitch tops of sleeves to sides of body. Place centre of cast-on edge of collar at centre back of neck, then bring ends of collar to front and tuck into top of waistband of skirt; stitch in place. Stitch button to centre front.

Cut strands of buttercup-yellow yarn, lay them across the top of the head and stitch in place down centre using matching yarn and backstitch. Join ends of crown to form a ring, then stitch this on top of head.

Use various colours of yarn to embroider features. For mouth, stitch a single horizontal stitch in pink, then couch with short vertical stitches. Stitch two horizontal short stitches in white for each eye, then, with blue yarn, stitch a small stitch vertically across the white strands. Outline the top of each eye in backstitch, and embroider pupils and nostrils using black embroidery thread. (See pages 152–3 for more details about embroidering facial features.)

Most people will see this frog simply as a pond-dwelling amphibian but any passing princesses will view him as a potential husband and kiss him in the hope of a magical transformation.

Frog prince

Materials

4-ply knitting yarn in sage green (A) and white (B), plus small amounts of black and red
Pair of 2.75mm (UK12:US2) knitting needles
2 × double-pointed 2.75mm (UK12:US2) knitting needles
Tapestry needle
Polyester toy filling

Size

Frog measures approximately 2½in (6.25cm) in length.

Tension

See page 142

Body and head (made in one piece)

Using 2.75mm needles and A, cast on 24 sts.

Row 1: K each st tbl.

Knit 27 rows.

Row 29: K3, (k3tog, k2) 3 times, k3tog, k3 (16 sts).

Knit 3 rows.

Row 33: K3, (incl in next st, k2) 3 times, incl in next st, k3 (20 sts).

Row 34: K2, (incl in next st, k2) 6 times (26 sts).

Row 35: K to end.

Row 36: K2, (incl in next st, k6) 3 times, incl in next st, k2 (30 sts).

Knit 4 rows.

Row 41: K2, (k2tog, k4) 4 times, k2tog, k2 (25 sts).

Row 42: K to end.

Row 43: K1, (k2tog, k5) 3 times, k2tog, k1 (21 sts).

Row 44: K to end.

Row 45: K2, (k2tog, k3) 3 times, k2tog, k2 (17 sts).

Row 46: K3, (k2tog, k1) 3 times, k2tog, k3 (13 sts).

Row 47: K2, (k3tog) 3 times, k2.

Cut yarn, leaving a tail, and thread through rem 7 sts.

Arms and hands (make 2)

Using 2.75mm needles and A, cast on 16 sts.

Row 1: K each st tbl.

Hand

(Turn and cast on 8 sts; turn and cast off 8 sts) 3 times; cast off rem sts.

Eyes

Using two 2.75mm double-pointed needles and A, cast on 5 sts.

Row 1: K5, do not turn but slide sts to other end of needle.

Rep this row 39 times more, cast off.

Eyeballs (make 2)

Using 2.75mm needles and B, cast on 16 sts, cast off.

Making up

Stitch back seam of body and head. Stuff head with polyester filling. Stitch a running stitch around neckline and pull up tightly.

Attach arms to body, just below head. Use yarn end between 'fingers' to neaten the hand, gathering up the stitches that form each finger so that they are more rigid.

To create eyes, stitch centre of cord to centre top of head, then roll up either end towards centre and secure with a few firm stitches. Curl the whites of the eyes into circles and stitch in place. Thread a tapestry needle with black yarn and embroider pupils in satin stitch. Thread needle with red yarn and embroider one long horizontal stitch across centre of face for mouth, then oversew this stitch with couching stitches to create a wide mouth. Embroider nostrils using black yarn. (See pages 152–3 for more details about embroidering facial features.)

Every story needs its villain — and that's where Wilma makes
her dramatic entrance. With her scary face and magic broomstick,
she is the mean and nasty member of the group.

Wilma witch

Materials

4-ply knitting yarn in black (A), apple green (B), purple (C),
   plum (D), chocolate (E) and mustard (F), plus small
   amounts of grey and red
Pair of 2.75mm (UK12:US2) knitting needles
Pair of 2.25mm (UK13:US1) knitting needles
Narrow plastic drinking straw for the broomstick
Tapestry needle
Polyester toy stuffing

Size

Wilma's body measures approximately 2½in (6.25cm)
in length.

Tension

See page 142

Special abbreviations

MB1: increase by knitting into front, back, front, back and front of stitch, turn and p5; turn and k5; turn and p5; turn and pass second, third, fourth and fifth st over first st, then k into the back of this st.

MB2: increase by knitting into front, back and front of st, turn and p3, turn and pass second and third sts over first st then k into the back of this st.

Body and head
(made in one piece)

Using 2.75mm needles and A, cast on 20 sts.

Row 1: K each st tbl.

Row 2: P to end.

Row 3: K to end.

Row 4: P to end.

Row 5: K1, (yfwd, k2tog) 9 times, k1. Beg with a p row, work 23 rows in stocking stitch.

Row 29: K4, [(k2tog) twice, k4] twice (16 sts).

Row 30: P to end; cut A and join in B.

Row 31: Using B, k to end.

Row 32: P to end.

Row 33: K6, (inc1 in next st) 4 times, k6 (20 sts).

Row 34: P to end.

Row 35: K10, pick up loop in front of next st and MB1, k10 (21 sts).

Row 36: P to end.

Row 37: K to end.

Row 38: P to end.

Row 39: K10, MB2 in next st, k10.

Row 40: P to end.
Beg with a k row, work 4 rows in stocking stitch.

Row 45: (K2tog) 5 times, k1, (k2tog) 5 times (11 sts).

Row 46: (P2tog) twice, p3tog, (p2tog) twice; cut yarn and thread through rem 5 sts.

Skirt

Using 2.75mm needles and C, cast on 40 sts.

Row 1: K each st tbl.

Row 2: P to end.

Row 3: K to end.

Row 4: P to end.

Row 5: K1, (yfwd, k2tog) 19 times, k1. Beg with a p row, work 13 rows in stocking stitch.

Row 19: (K2tog) 20 times (20 sts).

Row 20: P to end.

Row 21: K to end.
Cast off knitwise.

Arms and sleeves
(make 2)

Using 2.75mm needles and B, cast on 4 sts.

Row 1: K each st tbl.

Row 2: Inc1 in each st (8 sts).
Beg with a p row, work 3 rows in stocking stitch; cut B and join in C.

Row 6: Using C, cast on 4 sts, k to end (12 sts).

Row 7: Cast on 4 sts, k to end (16 sts).
Beg with a k row, continue in stocking stitch for 16 rows, decreasing 1 st at each end of seventh, eleventh and fifteenth rows (10 sts). Cast off.

Shawl

Using 2.25mm needles and D, cast on 1 st.

Row 1: K into front, back and front of this st (3 sts).
Cont in garter stitch (k every row), inc 1 st at each end of every row until there are 29 sts. Cast off.

Hat

Using 2.75mm needles and A, cast on 22 sts.

Row 1: K each st tbl.

Row 2: P to end.

Row 3: K1, k2tog, k to last 3 sts, k2tog,

k1 (20 sts).
Rep rows 2 and 3 until 6 sts remain.
Next row: P to end.
Next row: (K2tog) 3 times (3 sts).
Next row: P to end.
Next row: K3tog; fasten off.

Hat brim
Using 2.25mm needles and A, cast on 4 sts.
Knit 68 rows. Cast off.

Making up the witch
At base of body, fold first few rows to wrong side along eyelet row and stitch in place to create a picot hem. Stitch back seam of body and head. Run a length of yarn through the stitches at neckline, stuff head and draw up yarn to close opening and shape neck.

At base of skirt, fold first few rows to wrong side along eyelet row and stitch in place to create a picot hem. Stitch back seam of skirt; run a length of yarn through the stitches at waistline, slip on to body and stitch top of skirt to body at waistline, pulling up yarn to tighten top of skirt slightly. Stitch seams on each arm and sleeve piece, adding a little stuffing to sleeves if you wish, and stitch tops of sleeves to sides of body.

Place centre of cast-off edge of shawl at centre back of neck, then bring ends of shawl to front, cross over and stitch in place. Cut strands of grey yarn, lay them across the top of the head and stitch in place down centre using matching yarn and backstitch.

Stitch seam on hat and stitch to top of head, then stitch two short ends of hat brim together; run a gathering stitch around one long edge and pull up to fit head; stitch in place around bottom edge of hat.

To create the crinkly effect on the hair, use the point of the tapestry needle to separate the strands of grey yarn, running the needle from the top of each strand, where it emerges from the hat brim, to the tip. Trim yarn ends to the desired length.

Neaten and shape chin using matching yarn. Use black yarn to embroider eyes and eyebrows. For the mouth, stitch two horizontal stitches in crimson, then one horizontal stitch in black in between the two. (See pages 152–3 for more details about embroidering facial features.)

Broomstick
This is an essential piece of kit for any witch – but there are other characters in this book who would find a broom very useful, too. You could make one for the Milkmaid on page 47, Mrs Moppet on page 137 or maybe for Capability clown on page 29.

Using 2.25mm knitting needles and E, cast on 28 sts.
Row 1: K each st tbl.
Knit 2 rows. Cast off.

Making up the broomstick
To make up the broomstick, cut a 3¼in (8cm) length from a narrow plastic drinking straw, wrap the strip of knitting around it and oversew cast-on and cast-off edges together. Bind short lengths of yarn F around one end.

Walter the Wizard – Wally to his close friends – likes nothing better than to pass on his wisdom and knowledge to others. Perhaps you could appoint him head of your very own wizarding school and make up all kinds of stories.

Wally wizard

Materials

4-ply knitting yarn in purple (A), fawn (B) and white (C), plus a small amount of black

Pair of 2.75mm (UK12:US2) knitting needles

Tapestry needle

Polyester toy stuffing

Size

Wally's body measures approximately 2½in (6.25cm) in length.

Tension

See page 142

Body and head (made in one piece)

Using 2.75mm needles and A, cast on 20 sts.

Row 1: K each st tbl.

Row 2: P to end.

Row 3: K to end.

Rows 4–6: P to end.

Beg with a k row, work 22 rows in stocking stitch.

Row 29: K4, [(k2tog) twice, k4] twice (16 sts).

Row 30: P to end; cut A and join in B.

Beg with a k row, work 4 rows in stocking stitch.

Row 35: K6, (inc1 in next st) 4 times, k6 (20 sts).

Beg with a p row, work 11 rows in stocking stitch.

Row 47: (K2tog) 10 times (10 sts).

Row 48: P to end.

Row 49: (K2tog) 5 times.

Cut yarn and thread through rem 5 sts.

Robe

Using 2.75mm needles and A, cast on 42 sts.

Row 1: K each st tbl.

Rows 2–3: K to end.

Beg with a p row, work 3 rows in stocking stitch.

Row 7: K1, sl1, psso, k to last 3 sts, k2tog, k1.

Row 8: P to end.

Rep rows 7 and 8 until 18 sts rem.

Purl 3 rows.

Cast off knitwise.

Hat

Using 2.75mm needles and A, cast on 24 sts.

Beg with a p row, work 9 rows in stocking stitch.

Row 10: K1, sl1, psso, k to last 3 sts, k2tog, k1.

Row 11: P to end.

Rep rows 10 and 11 until 4 sts rem.

Next row: (K2tog) twice.

Cast off rem 2 sts.

Making up

At base of body, fold first few rows to wrong side along purl ridge and stitch in place to create a hem. Stitch back seam of body and head. Run a length of yarn through the stitches at neckline, stuff head and draw up yarn to close opening and shape neck.

Wrap robe around body, with last few rows forming collar. Run a length of yarn through the stitches below the

collar and draw up to gather slightly, then stitch robe in place. Add a length of yarn at either side of collar at front and tie in a neat bow.

Cut strands of yarn C and lay them across the top of the head, then stitch in place down centre using matching yarn and backstitch. Stitch the seam on the hat and roll up the brim, then place it on top of the head, with the seam at the back. Make sure the strands of hair are evenly distributed around the head, then stitch the hat in place.

To create the crinkly effect on the hair, use the point of the tapestry needle to separate the strands of yarn, running the needle from the top of each strand, where it emerges from the hat brim, to the tip. Trim the yarn ends to the desired length.

Use yarn B to embroider a nose and two ears in bullion stitch, then use black yarn to embroider eyes and mouth, and white yarn for a little moustache. (See pages 152–3 for more details about embroidering facial features.)

To make a wand for Walter, why not use the pattern for the Fairy godmother's wand on page 83, using black or purple or your own choice of colours?

Flossie has the power to make your wishes come true
– as long as you are good and kind. She's the sweetest fairy godmother
of them all and can't wait to be a part of your fairytale fantasies.

Fairy godmother

Materials

4-ply knitting yarn in apple green (A), beige (B), bright pink (C),
   pink (D), sky blue (E), mustard (F), white (G), ivory (H)
   and crimson (I), plus small amounts of black, apple
   green and bright pink

Pair of 2.75mm (UK12:US2) knitting needles

Pair of 2.25mm (UK13:US1) knitting needles

2 x 2.25mm (UK13:US1) double-pointed knitting needles

Tapestry needle

Polyester toy stuffing

Small wooden bead for wand (optional)

2in (5cm) of narrow plastic drinking straw for wand

Size

Flossie's body measures approximately 2½in (6.25cm)
in length.

Tension

See page 142

Body and head (made in one piece)

Using 2.75mm needles and A, cast on 20 sts.

Row 1: K each st tbl.
Row 2: P to end.
Row 3: K to end.
Row 4: P to end.
Row 5: K1, (yfwd, k2tog) 9 times, k1.
Beg with a p row, work 23 rows in stocking stitch.
Row 29: K4, [(k2tog) twice, k4] twice (16 sts).
Row 30: P to end; cut A and join in B.
Row 31: Using B, k to end.
Row 32: P to end.
Row 33: K6, (incl in next st) 4 times, k6 (20 sts).
Beg with a p row, work 5 rows in stocking stitch.
Row 39: K9, (incl in next st) twice, k9 (22 sts).
Row 40: P to end.
Row 41: K9, sl1, k1, psso, k2tog, k9.
Beg with a p row, work 3 rows in stocking stitch.
Row 45: (K2tog) 10 times (10 sts).
Row 46: (P2tog) 5 times; cut yarn and thread through rem 5 sts.

Skirt

Using 2.75mm needles and C, cast on 40 sts.

Row 1: K each st tbl.
Row 2: P to end.
Row 3: K to end.
Row 4: P to end.
Row 5: K1, (yfwd, k2tog) 19 times, k1.
Row 6: P to end.
Row 7: K to end; cut C and join in D.
Row 8: Using D, p to end of row; cut D and join in E.
Beg with a k row, work 10 rows in stocking stitch.
Row 19: (K2tog) 20 times (20 sts).
Row 20: P to end.
Row 21: K to end.
Cast off knitwise.

Arms and sleeves (make 2)

Using 2.75mm needles and B, cast on 4 sts.

Row 1: Incl in each st (8 sts).
Beg with a p row, work 5 rows in stocking stitch; cut B and join in E.
Using C, work 6 rows in stocking stitch.
Row 13: Incl in each st (16 sts).
Beg with a p row, work 3 rows in stocking stitch.
Row 17: (K2tog) 8 times (8 sts).
Cast off purlwise.

Bodice

Using 2.75mm needles and E, cast on 40 sts.

Row 1: K each st tbl.
Row 2: P to end.
Row 3: K to end.
Cast off.

Bun

Using two 2.25mm double-pointed needles and F, cast on 3 sts.

Row 1: K3; do not turn but, with RS facing, slide sts to other end of needle. Rep row 1 40 times more. Cast off.

Wings (make 2)

With 2.25mm needles and G, cast on 5 sts.

Row 1: Incl in each st (10 sts).
Row 2 (and each WS row): P to end.
Row 3: Incl in each st (20 sts).
Row 5: (K1, incl) 10 times (30 sts).
Row 7: (K2, incl) 10 times (40 sts).
Cast off knitwise.

Belt

Using 2.25mm knitting needles and C, cast on 24 sts.

Row 1: K each st tbl.
Cast off, knitting each st tbl.

Making up Flossie

At base of body, fold first few rows to wrong side along eyelet row and stitch to create a picot hem. Stitch back seam of body and head. Run yarn through the stitches at neckline, stuff head and draw up yarn to close and shape neck.

At base of skirt, fold first few rows to wrong side along eyelet row and stitch in place to create a picot hem. Stitch back seam of skirt; run a length of yarn through the stitches at waistline, slip on to body and stitch top of skirt to body at waistline, pulling up yarn to tighten top of skirt slightly. Stitch seams on each arm and sleeve piece, adding a little stuffing to sleeves if you wish, and stitch tops of sleeves to sides of body.

Place centre of cast-on edge of bodice at centre back of neck, then bring ends of bodice to front and stitch to waistband of skirt. Wrap belt around waist and stitch ends together. Run a length of yarn along side edges on each wing and pull up to gather into a round shape, then stitch in place with gathered edges meeting at centre back.

Using mustard yarn, stitch hair in satin stitch, taking stitches from nape of neck to crown of head. Roll up bun to form a cone-shaped coil and stitch to top of head. Use yarn B to embroider nose in satin stitch and ears in bullion stitch. Use black yarn for two beady eyes and bright pink for a small mouth. (See pages 152–3 for more details about embroidering facial features.)

Wand

Every Fairy Godmother needs a wand to help cast spells and grant wishes. You can also use this pattern to make a wand for the wizard on page 77, if you like.

Stem

Using 2.25mm needles and G, cast on 16 sts.

Row 1: K each st tbl.

Knit 3 rows.

Cast off, knitting each st tbl.

Ball

Using 2.25mm needles and G, cast on 5 sts.

Row 1: P to end.

Row 2: Cast on 1 st, k to end (6 sts).

Row 3: Cast on 1 st, p to end (7 sts).

Row 4: Cast on 1 st, k to end (8 sts).

Row 5: Cast on 1 st, p to end (9 sts). Beg with a k row, work 2 rows in stocking stitch.

Row 8: Cast off 1 st, k to end (8 sts).

Row 9: Cast off 1 st, p to end (7 sts).

Row 10: Cast off 1 st, k to end (6 sts).

Row 11: Cast off 1 st, p to end.

Cast off rem 5 sts.

Making up the wand

Wrap the strip of knitting around the 2in (5cm) length of drinking straw and oversew cast-on and cast-off edges together to form the stem of the wand. Stitch side seam on ball, inserting a round bead or some stuffing, then stitch to one end of stem. Tie strands of coloured yarn around stem, just below ball.

Toadstool

Stem and cap
(made in one piece)

Using 2.25mm double-pointed needles and H, cast on 9 sts and divide equally over three needles.

Round 1: K each st tbl.

Round 2: P to end of round.

Knit 14 rounds.

Round 17: Inc1 in each st (18 sts).

Round 18: (K1, inc1) 9 times (27 sts).

Round 19: (K2, inc1) 9 times (36 sts).

Round 20: (K3, inc1) 9 times (45 sts); cut H and join in I.

Round 21: Using I, (K4, inc1) 9 times (54 sts).

Knit 3 rounds.

Round 25: (K4, k2tog) 9 times (45 sts).

Knit 2 rounds.

Round 28: (K3, k2tog) 9 times (36 sts).

Round 29: K to end.

Round 30: (K2, k2tog) 9 times (27 sts).

Round 31: (K1, k2tog) 9 times (18 sts).

Round 32: (K2tog) 9 times.

Cut yarn and thread through rem 9 sts.

Making up the toadstool

Stuff toadstool through hole in top of cap, then pull up yarn and stitch hole closed. Thread tapestry needle with white yarn and embroider small spots in satin stitch over cap.

A pixie can play all kinds of parts in your storytelling.
Legend has it that pixies lead travellers astray – but there
are also rumours that pixies help with the housework.

Pixie Pete

Materials

4-ply knitting yarn in sage green (A), ivory (B) and purple (C),
   plus small amounts of gold, geranium red and black
Pair of 2.75mm (UK12:US2) knitting needles
Pair of 2.25mm (UK13:US1) knitting needles
Tapestry needle
Polyester toy filling

Size

Pete's body measures approximately 2½in (6.25cm) in length.

Tension

See page 142

Body and head
(made in one piece)

Using 2.75mm needles and A, cast on 20 sts.

Row 1: K each st tbl.

Row 2: P to end.

Row 3: K to end.

Row 4: P to end.

Row 5: K1, (yfwd, k2tog) 9 times, k1.

Beg with a p row, work 21 rows in stocking stitch.

Row 27: K4, (k2tog) twice, k4, (k2tog) twice, k4 (16 sts).

Row 28: P to end; cut A and join in B.

Row 29: Using B, k to end.

Row 30: P to end.

Row 31: K6, (inc1 in next st) 4 times, k6 (20 sts).

Beg with a p row, work 9 rows in stocking stitch.

Row 41: (K2tog) to end; cut yarn and thread through rem 10 sts.

Tunic

Using 2.75mm needles and A, cast on 24 sts.

Row 1: K each st tbl.

Row 2: P to end.

Row 3: K to end.

Row 4: P to end.

Row 5: K1, (yfwd, k2tog) 11 times, k1.

Beg with a p row, work 13 rows in stocking stitch.

Row 19: K5, (k2tog) twice, k6, (k2tog) twice, k5 (20 sts).

Row 20: P to end.

Row 21: K4, (k2tog) twice, k4, (k2tog) twice, k4.

Row 22: P to end; break yarn and thread through rem 16 sts.

Hands and arms
(make 2)

Using 2.75mm needles and B, cast on 8 sts.

Row 1: P to end.

Row 2: K to end.

Row 3: P to end; cut B and join in A. Using A and beg with a k row, work 10 rows in stocking stitch. Cast off.

Hat

Using 2.75mm needles and A, cast on 24 sts.

Row 1: K each st tbl.

Beg with a p row, work 3 rows in stocking stitch.

Row 5: K1, (yfwd, k2tog) 11 times, k1. Beg with a p row, work 9 rows in stocking stitch.

Row 15: (K1, k2tog) 8 times (16 sts).

Row 16: P to end.

Row 17: (K2tog) 8 times (8 sts).

Row 18: P to end.

Row 19: (K2tog) 4 times (4 sts).

Row 20: P to end.

Row 21: (K2tog) twice.

Cast off rem 2 sts.

Belt

Using 2.25mm needles and C, cast on 20 sts.

Row 1: K each st tbl.

Cast off knitwise.

Ears (make 2)

Using 2.25mm needles and B, cast on 7 sts.

Row 1: P to end.

Row 2: K2tog, k3, k2tog (5 sts).

Row 3: P to end.

Row 4: K2tog, k1, k2tog (3 sts).

Row 5: P to end.

Row 6: Sl1, k2tog, psso; fasten off.

Neck ruff

Using 2.25mm needles and A, cast on 6 sts using cable method.

Row 1: Cast off 4 sts, k to end.

Row 2: K2, turn.

Row 3: Cast on 4 sts, cast off 4 sts, k to end.

Rep rows 2 and 3 until you have made 8 'petals'.

Cast off rem 2 sts.

Making up

At base of body, fold first few rows to wrong side along eyelet row and stitch in place to create a picot hem. Stitch back seam of body and head. Run a length of yarn through the stitches at neckline, stuff head and draw up yarn to close opening and shape neck.

At base of tunic, fold first few rows to wrong side along eyelet row and stitch in place to create a picot hem. Stitch back seam of tunic; run a length of yarn through the stitches at neckline, slip on to body and stitch top of tunic to body, pulling up yarn to fit snugly around neck.

Stitch seams on each arm and sleeve piece, pushing yarn ends into sleeves to add a little padding, then stitch tops of sleeves to sides of body. Run a length of yarn through the stitches along the straight edge of the neck ruff, pull up to fit neck and stitch in place, with ends meeting at centre back of neck. Fold each ear in half and stitch to sides of head.

Fold under first few rows of hat to create brim, then stitch seam and stuff lightly if you wish. Place hat on top of head and stitch firmly in place. Wrap belt around waist and stitch ends together. Thread a length of gold yarn in tapestry needle and embroider a belt buckle. To do this, first stitch four straight stitches, two vertical and two horizontal, to form a square, then whipstitch all round.

For the mouth, stitch a fly stitch in geranium red. Use black yarn to embroider the eyes. Use yarn B to embroider a nose in satin stitch. (See pages 152–3 for more details about embroidering facial features.)

The high seas

Sidney the sailor is seeking adventure. He has all his worldly goods packed in his duffel bag and is ready to jump aboard the next ship that sets sail for foreign shores.

Sailor Sid

Materials

4-ply knitting yarn in white (A), pale peach (B), navy (C)
 and buff (D), plus small amounts of tangerine,
  rose pink and black
Pair of 2.75mm (UK12:US2) knitting needles
Pair of 2.25mm (UK13:US1) knitting needles
4 x 2.25mm (UK13:US1) double-pointed knitting needles
Tapestry needle
Polyester toy filling

Size

Sid's body measures approximately 2½in (6.25cm) in length.

Tension

See page 142

Body and head (made in one piece)

Using 2.75mm needles and A, cast on 20 sts.

Row 1: K each st tbl.

Row 2: P to end.

Row 3: K to end.

Rows 4–6: P to end.

Beg with a k row, work 20 rows in stocking stitch.

Row 27: K4, (k2tog) twice, k4, (k2tog) twice, k4 (16 sts).

Row 28: P to end; cut A and join in B.

Row 29: Using B, k to end.

Row 30: P to end.

Row 31: K6, (incl in next st) 4 times, k6 (20 sts).

Beg with a p row, work 9 rows in stocking stitch.

Row 41: (K2tog) to end; cut yarn and thread through rem 10 sts.

Tunic

Using 2.75mm needles and A, cast on 24 sts.

Row 1: K each st tbl.

Row 2: P to end.

Row 3: K to end.

Rows 4–6: P to end.

Beg with a k row, work 12 rows in stocking stitch.

Row 19: K5, (k2tog) twice, k6, (k2tog) twice, k5 (20 sts).

Row 20: P to end.

Row 21: K4, (k2tog) twice, k4, (k2tog) twice, k4.

Row 22: P to end; break yarn and thread through rem 16 sts.

Hands and arms (make 2)

Using 2.75mm needles and B, cast on 4 sts.

Row 1: P to end.

Row 2: Incl knitwise in each st (8 sts).

Row 3: P to end.

Row 4: K to end

Row 5: P to end; cut B and join in A.

Rows 6–8: Using A, k to end.

Beg with a p row, work 9 rows in stocking stitch; cast off.

Hat

Using set of four 2.25mm double-pointed needles and C, cast on 24 sts and divide equally over three needles.

Round 1: K to end; cut yarn C and join in A.

Round 2: Incl in each st (48 sts).

Round 3: (K6, k2tog) 6 times (42 sts).

Round 4: (K5, k2tog) 6 times (36 sts).

Round 5: (K4, k2tog) 6 times (30 sts).

Round 6: (K3, k2tog) 6 times (24 sts).

Round 7: (K2, k2tog) 6 times (18 sts).

Round 8: (K1, k2tog) 6 times (12 sts).

Round 9: (K2tog) 6 times.

Cut yarn and thread through rem 6 sts.

Collar

Using 2.25mm needles and C, cast on 12 sts.

Knit 6 rows.

Row 7: K6; turn and transfer rem 6 sts to a safety pin.

Row 8: Cast off 1 st, k to end (5 sts).

Rows 9–11: K to end.

Row 12: Cast off 1 st, k to end (4 sts).

Rows 13–15: K to end.

Row 16: Cast off 1 st, k to end (3 sts).

Rows 17–19: K to end.

Row 20: Cast off 1 st, k to end (2 sts).

Rows 21–23: K to end.

Cast off.

Cut yarn and rejoin to sts on safety pin, then work 2nd side to match, reversing shaping.

Making up the sailor

At base of body, fold first few rows to wrong side along purl ridge and stitch in place to create a hem. Stitch back seam of body and head. Run a length of yarn through the stitches at neckline, stuff head and draw up yarn to close opening and shape neck.

At base of tunic, fold first few rows to wrong side along purl ridge and stitch in place to create a hem. Stitch back seam of tunic; run a length of yarn through the stitches at neckline, slip on to body and stitch top of tunic to body, pulling up yarn to fit snugly around neck. Stitch seams on each arm and sleeve piece, pushing yarn ends into sleeves to add a little padding, then stitch tops of sleeves to sides of body.

Stitch a few strands of tangerine yarn to front of head, to form a little fringe of hair. Pull tail of yarn at top of hat to close gap. Place hat on top of head, adding a little stuffing if you wish, then stitch firmly in place, with fringe poking out from brim. Trim ends of fringe. Wrap collar around neck and stitch ends together. Attach to back of neck with a few discreet stitches.

Use yarn B to create ears in bullion stitch and a satin-stitch nose. For the mouth, stitch a small straight stitch in rose pink. Use black yarn to embroider eyes and eyebrows. (See pages 152–3 for more details about embroidering facial features.)

Duffel bag

Sailor Sid needs somewhere to stash all his stuff, and this classic duffel bag is just the thing. You could make these for some of the other characters, too: a green one for Pixie Pete (page 85) and a red one for the Ringmaster (page 25) to store his whip and ball, perhaps?

Using set of four 2.25mm double-pointed needles and C, cast on 30 sts and divide equally over three needles.
Round 1: K to end.
Round 2: (Yfwd, k2tog) to end of round.
Knit 21 rounds.

Round 24: (K3, k2tog) 6 times (24 sts).
Round 25: (K2, k2tog) 6 times (18 sts).
Round 26: (K1, k2tog) 6 times (12 sts).
Round 27: (K2tog) 6 times.
Cut yarn and thread through rem 6 sts.

Making up the duffel bag

Make a twisted cord (see page 150) from yarn D. Weave this cord in and out of the eyelet holes, then stitch ends to base of bag.

Ahoy there! Meet Pandora, the swashbuckling pirate.
Life ashore as a lily-livered landlubber didn't suit this bold maiden,
so she has taken to the high seas, looking for adventure.

Pandora pirate

Materials

4-ply knitting yarn in Prussian blue (A), pale peach (B),
geranium red (C), white (D) and black, plus a small
amount of raspberry
Pair of 2.75mm (UK12:US2) knitting needles
Pair of 2.25mm (UK13:US1) knitting needles
Tapestry needle
Polyester toy filling

Size

Pandora's body measures approximately 2½in (6.25cm)
in length.

Tension

See page 142

Body and head
(made in one piece)
Using 2.75mm needles and A, cast on 20 sts.

Row 1: K each st tbl.

Row 2: P to end.

Row 3: K to end.

Rows 4–6: P to end.

Beg with a k row, work 20 rows in stocking stitch.

Row 27: K4, (k2tog) twice, k4, (k2tog) twice, k4 (16 sts).

Row 28: P to end; cut A and join in B.

Row 29: Using B, k to end.

Row 30: P to end.

Row 31: K6, (inc1 in next st) 4 times, k6 (20 sts).

Beg with a p row, work 9 rows in stocking stitch.

Row 41: (K2tog) to end; cut yarn and thread through rem 10 sts.

Jumper
Using 2.75mm needles and C, cast on 24 sts.

Row 1: K each st tbl.

Row 2: P to end.

Row 3: K to end.

Row 4: P to end.

Row 5: K1, (yfwd, k2tog) 11 times, k1.

Row 6: P to end; do not cut yarn C but join in D.

Beg with a k row and yarn D, work 2 rows in stocking stitch, then work in 2-row stripes, alternating colours, for a

further 8 rows.

Row 17: Using C, k5, (k2tog) twice, k6, (k2tog) twice, k5 (20 sts).

Row 18: P to end; cut yarn C.

Row 19: Using D, k4, (k2tog) twice, k4, (k2tog) twice, k4 (16 sts).

Row 20: P to end; break yarn and thread through rem 16 sts.

Hands and arms
(make 2)
Using 2.75mm needles and B, cast on 4 sts.

Row 1: P to end.

Row 2: Inc1 knitwise in each st (8 sts).

Row 3: P to end.

Row 4: K to end

Row 5: P to end; cut B and join in C.

Row 6: Using C, k to end.

Row 7: P to end; do not cut yarn C but join in D.

Beg with a k row and yarn D, work 2 rows in stocking stitch, then work in 2-row stripes, alternating colours, for a further 10 rows.
Cast off in yarn C.

Bandanna
Using 2.25mm needles and C, cast on 1 st.

Row 1: K.

Row 2: P.

Row 3: Inc2 (3 sts).

Beg with a p row, work 11 rows in stocking stitch.

Row 15: K1, inc1, k1 (4 sts).

Beg with a p row, work 11 rows in stocking stitch.

Row 27: K1, k2tog, k1 (3 sts).

Beg with a p row, work 11 rows in stocking stitch.

Row 39: K3 tog.

Row 40: P.

Cut yarn and fasten off.

Making up
At base of body, fold first few rows to wrong side along purl ridge and stitch in place to create a hem. Stitch back seam of body and head. Run a length of yarn through the stitches at neckline, stuff head and draw up yarn to close opening and shape neck. At base of jumper, fold first few rows to wrong side along eyelet row and stitch in place to create a picot hem. Stitch back

seam of jumper; run a length of yarn through the stitches at neckline, slip on to body and stitch top of tunic to body, pulling up yarn to fit snugly around neck. Stitch seams on each arm and sleeve piece, pushing yarn ends into sleeves to add a little padding, then stitch tops of sleeves to sides of body.

Use yarn B to create ears in bullion stitch and a satin-stitch nose. For the mouth, stitch a small straight stitch in raspberry. Use black yarn to embroider eyes and eyebrows. (See pages 152–3 for more details about embroidering facial features.)

Make a bundle of black yarn and stitch to top of head, then stitch in place all round circumference of head, above ears. Embroider small white dots all over bandanna then wrap bandanna around head to hold hair in place, allowing a few strands of hair to stick out above the bandanna at the front, and secure the ends of the bandanna at the point where they overlap.

Is he the terror of the oceans or simply a benign buccaneer?
Captain Constantine Cutlass, 'Tiny' to his friends,
is ready to take you on a pirate adventure.

Captain Cutlass

Materials

4-ply knitting yarn in Prussian blue (A), geranium red (B),
  white (C), beige (D), plum (E), black (F) and gold (G),
  plus small amounts of pink and turquoise
One 'diamond' button
Pair of 2.75mm (UK12:US2) knitting needles
Pair of 2.25mm (UK13:US1) knitting needles
Tapestry needle
Needle and thread
Polyester toy stuffing

Size

The Captain's body measures approximately 2½in (6.25cm)
in length.

Tension

See page 142

Body and head (in one piece)

Using 2.25mm needles and A, cast on 24 sts.

Row 1: K to end.

Row 2: P to end.

Rows 3–4: K to end.

Row 5: (K1, p1) 12 times.

Rep row 5 11 times more.

Cut yarn A and join in B; change to 2.75mm needles.

Sash

Using B and beg with a k row, work 4 rows in stocking stitch; cut yarn B and join in C.

Torso and head

Using C and beg with a k row, work 8 rows in stocking stitch.

Row 29: K1, k2tog, (k2, k2tog) 5 times, k1 (18 sts).

Row 30: P to end; cut yarn C and join in D.

Row 31: Using D, k to end.

Row 32: P to end.

Row 33: K1, inc1, (k2, inc1) 5 times, k1 (24 sts).

Beg with a p row, work 11 rows in stocking stitch.

Row 45: (K2tog) 12 times (12 sts).

Row 46: (P2tog) 6 times.

Cut yarn and thread through rem 6 sts.

Arms (make 2)

Using 2.75mm needles and D, cast on 4 sts.

Row 1: K to end.

Row 2: P to end.

Row 3: Inc1 in each st (8 sts).

Row 4: P to end.

Row 5: K to end.

Row 6: P to end; cut D and join in C.

Rows 7–9: Using D, k to end.

Beg with a p row, work 15 rows in stocking stitch.

Cast off.

Jacket

Main part

Using 2.75mm needles and E, cast on 28 sts.

Row 1 (WS): K each st tbl.

Row 2: K to end.

Row 3: K1, p to last st, k1.

Rep rows 2 and 3 eight times more.

Row 20: K4, [(k2tog) twice, k4] 3 times (22 sts).

Row 21: P to end.

Row 22: (K2tog) 11 times (11 sts).

Row 23: P to end.

Cast off.

Sleeves (make 2)

Using 2.75mm needles and E, cast on 11 sts.

Row 1 (WS): K each st tbl.

Row 2: K to end.

Beg with a p row, work 11 rows in stocking stitch.

Row 14: K1, sl1, k1, psso, k5, k2tog, k1 (9 sts).

Row 15: P to end.

Row 16: K1, sl1, k1, psso, k3, k2tog, k1 (7 sts).

Row 17: P to end.

Cast off.

Collar

Using 2.75mm needles and C, cast on 12 sts.

Row 1: K to end.

Row 2: Inc1 in first st, k10, inc1 in last st (14 sts).

Cast off.

Hat (made in two pieces)

Crown

Using 2.25mm needles and F, cast on 1 st and k into front, back, front, back and front of this st (5 sts).

Row 1: Inc1 in each st (10 sts).

Row 2: P to end.

Row 3: (K1, inc1) 5 times (15 sts).

Row 4: P to end.

Row 5: (K2, inc1) 5 times (20 sts).

Row 6: P to end.

Row 7: (K3, inc1) 5 times (25 sts).

Row 8: P to end.

Row 9: K to end.

Cast off knitwise.

Brim

Cast on 5 sts.

Knit 68 rows. Cast off.

Cuff bands (make 2)

Using 2.25mm needles and G, cast on 14 sts.
Row 1: K each st tbl.
Cast off.

Coat fastenings (make 2)

Using 2.25mm needles and G, cast on 5 sts.
Row 1: K each st tbl.
Cast off.

Nose

Using 2.25mm needles and D, cast on 5 sts.
Beg with a k row, work 6 rows in stocking stitch.
Cast off.

Eye patch

Using 2.25mm needles and F, cast on 3 sts.
Row 1: K each st tbl.
Row 2: K to end.
Row 3: Sl1, k2tog, psso.
Cast off.

Making up

At base of body, fold first few rows to wrong side along purl ridge and stitch in place to create a hem. Stitch back seam of body and head. Run a length of yarn through the stitches at neckline, stuff head and draw up yarn to close opening and shape neck.

Wrap jacket around body, placing the two side edges at centre front. Stitch about ½in (1cm) of these edges together, starting about 2 rows down from cast-off edge, and stitch coat fastenings across this join. Fold back edges below this point and stitch in place to form coat tails, then stitch cast-on edge of collar in place on top edge of jacket, around back of neck, and stitch collar points to front of jacket. Use a needle and thread to stitch button in centre of sash.

Stitch arm seams, stuffing with any yarn ends, then attach to top of main piece of jacket at shoulders. Stitch sleeve seams, slip each one over one of the arms and stitch in place, allowing the white purl ridge to show just below the jacket cuff. Stitch a cuff band on both cuffs, just above garter-stitch ridge.

Stitch seam on crown of hat and sew to top of head. Then stitch two short ends of hat brim together, run a gathering stitch around one long edge and pull up to fit head; stitch in place around bottom edge of crown; fold back brim at front and back. Make a small plume of turquoise yarn and stitch to one side of hat.

Create ears using beige yarn and bullion stitch. For nose, roll up, tucking in the cast-off edge and creating a tight cone with one end slightly thicker than the other. Stitch in place using tail of yarn, with thicker part at the base. Stitch eye patch in place and use yarn F to embroider a cord, an eye, a little moustache and a beard. Sew two small horizontal stitches for the mouth. (See pages 152–3 for more details about embroidering facial features.)

Stranded on a remote desert island with only a palm tree for shelter,
Crusoe survives on a diet of coconuts and fish, waiting patiently
to be rescued by a passing ship.

Castaway Crusoe

Materials

4-ply knitting yarn in fawn (A), buff (B), ivory (C), buttercup
  yellow (D), chocolate brown (E) and sage green (F),
  plus small amounts of geranium red, white and black
2 small white buttons
1 large button or plastic disc approximately 1¼in (3cm)
  in diameter for the palm tree
Pair of 2.75mm (UK12:US2) knitting needles
Tapestry needle
Polyester toy filling

Size

Crusoe's body measures approximately 2¼in (5.5cm)
in length.

Tension

See page 142

Body and head (made in one piece)

Using 2.75mm needles and A, cast on 20 sts.

Row 1: K each st tbl.

Row 2: P to end.

Row 3: K to end.

Row 4: P to end.

Row 5: K1, (yfwd, k2tog) 9 times, k1.

Beg with a p row, work 11 rows in stocking stitch; cut yarn, join in B and work a further 10 rows in stocking stitch.

Row 27: K4, (k2tog) twice, k4, (k2tog) twice, k4 (16 sts).

Row 28: P to end; cut A and join in B.

Row 29: Using B, k to end.

Row 30: P to end.

Row 31: K6, (inc1 in next st) 4 times, k6 (20 sts).

Beg with a p row, work 9 rows in stocking stitch.

Row 41: (K2tog) to end; cut yarn and thread through rem 10 sts.

Shirt

Using 2.75mm needles and C, (cast on 6 sts, cast off 3, return st on RH needle to LH needle) 8 times (24 sts).

Beg with a k row, work 12 rows in stocking stitch.

Row 13: K5, (k2tog) twice, k6, (k2tog) twice, k5 (20 sts).

Row 14: P to end.

Row 15: K4, (k2tog) twice, k4, (k2tog) twice, k4 (16 sts).

Row 16: P to end.

Cast off.

Hands and arms (make 2)

Using 2.75mm needles and B, cast on 4 sts.

Row 1: Inc1 in each st (8 sts).

Beg with a p row, work 19 rows in stocking stitch.

Cast off.

Sleeves (make 2)

Using 2.75mm needles and C, (cast on 4 sts, cast off 2, return st on RH needle to LH needle) 5 times (10 sts).

Row 1: K each st tbl.

Beg with a p row, work 7 rows in stocking stitch.

Row 9: K1, sl1, k1, psso, k4, k2tog, k1 (8 sts).

Row 10: P to end.

Row 11: K1, sl1, k1, psso, k2, k2tog, k1 (6 sts).

Cast off purlwise.

Making up the Castaway

At base of body, fold first few rows to wrong side along eyelet row and stitch in place to create a picot hem. Stitch back seam of body and head. Run a length of yarn through the stitches at neckline, stuff head and draw up yarn to close opening and shape neck.

Wrap shirt around body, placing the two side edges at centre front. Stitch edges together about ½in (1cm) down from cast-off edge and stitch button on top of this join; stitch another button to right shirt front just below first one. Fold back top edges of shirt for an open-necked effect, and stitch in place.

Stitch arm seams, stuffing with any remaining yarn ends, then fold over approximately ½in (1cm) at top of each one, to create extra bulk; attach to top of shirt at shoulders. Stitch sleeve seams, slip each one over one of the arms and stitch to shirt.

Using yarn B, make ears from bullion stitch and oversew the central line of stitches to form a nose. Use white yarn to embroider two pairs of horizontal straight stitches for eyes. Use black yarn to embroider a black stitch in the centre of each, and to embroider eyebrows. For mouth, stitch a fly stitch in geranium red. (See pages 152–3 for more details about embroidering facial features.)

For hair, tie about 12 strands of chocolate-brown yarn in a bundle and stitch to the top of the head. Fray the yarn ends using the point of a needle.

Attach individual strands around chin area, to make a beard, then fray these strands in the same way.

Palm tree

This is a great prop for creating a tropical island setting, and the other puppets – especially the Mermaid (page 107), the Pirate (page 95) and the Captain (page 99) – would be happy to shelter under the cool shade of the palm leaves.

Island and trunk

Using 2.75mm needles and D, cast on 40 sts.
Row 1: K each st tbl.
Row 2: P to end.
Row 3: K to end.
Row 4: P to end.

Row 5: (K2, k2tog) 10 times (30 sts).
Row 6: P to end.
Row 7: (K1, k2tog) 10 times (20 sts).
Row 8: P to end.
Row 9: (K2tog) 10 times (10 sts).
Row 10: P to end; cut D and join in E.
Using E, k 20 rows.
Row 31: (K2tog) 4 times.
Cast off rem 4 sts.

Palm leaves (make 4)

Using 2.75mm needles and F, cast on 16 sts.
Row 1 (WS): K each st tbl.
Row 2: K to end.
Row 3: P to end.
Row 4: K1, (yfwd, k2tog) to last st, k1.
Row 5: P to end.
Row 6: K to end.
Row 7: K to end.
Rep rows 2 to 6 once more.
Cast off knitwise.

Making up the palm tree

Stitch seam on island and trunk and stuff with polyester filling. Place a large button or plastic disc on top of stuffing at the base of the island. Stitch a running stitch all round cast-on edge and pull up to close gap and enclose button and stuffing. On each leaf, fold long edges to centre and stitch to back of central 'leaf vein' row, then attach leaves to top of trunk.

This stunning siren of the seas spends her days leisurely
basking on rocks, singing songs to passing sailors
and making beautiful necklaces from shells and pearls.

Pelagia mermaid

Materials

4-ply knitting yarn in ivory (A), ocean (B), lilac (C)
  and bright pink (D)
Pair of 2.75mm (UK12:US2) knitting needles
Pair of 2.25mm (UK13:US1) knitting needles
2 x 2.25mm (UK13:US1) double-pointed knitting needles
Safety pin
Tapestry needle
Polyester toy filling
Small pink glass beads
Needle and thread
Black embroidery thread

Size

Pelagia's body and tail measure approximately 4½in (11.5cm)
from neck to tip of tail.

Tension

See page 142

Body and head (made in one piece)

Using 2.75mm needles and A, cast on 20 sts.

Row 1: K to end.

Row 2: P to end.

Rep rows 1 and 2 four times more.

Row 11: K4, (k2tog) twice, k4, (k2tog) twice, k4 (16 sts).

Beg with a p row, work 3 rows in stocking stitch.

Row 15: K6, (incl in next st) 4 times, k6 (20 sts).

Beg with a p row, work 11 rows in stocking stitch.

Row 27: (K2tog) 10 times (10 sts).

Row 28: (P2tog) 5 times.

Cut yarn and thread through rem 5 sts.

Hands and arms (make 2)

Using 2.75mm needles and A, cast on 4 sts.

Row 1: K to end.

Row 2: P to end.

Row 3: Incl in each st (8 sts).

Beg with a p row, work 13 rows in stocking stitch.

Row 17: K1, incl in next st, K4, incl in next st, k1 (10 sts).

Beg with a p row, work 5 rows in stocking stitch.

Cast off.

Tail

Using 2.75mm needles and B, cast on 24 sts.

Row 1: K each st tbl.

Beg with a p row, work 7 rows in stocking stitch.

Row 9: K2, (k2tog, k4) 3 times, k2tog, k2 (20 sts).

Row 10: P to end.

Row 11: Cast off 4 sts, k to end (16 sts).

Row 12: Cast off 4 sts, p to end turn and cast on 4 sts.

Row 13: K to end, turn and cast on 4 sts (20 sts).

Beg with a p row, work 3 rows in stocking stitch.

Row 17: K2, k2tog, (k5, k2tog) twice, k2 (17 sts).

Beg with a p row, work 3 rows in stocking stitch.

Row 21: K2, k2tog, k9, k2tog, k2 (15 sts).

Beg with a p row, work 3 rows in stocking stitch.

Row 25: K2, k2tog, k7, k2tog, k2 (13 sts).

Row 26: P to end.

Row 27: K2, k2tog, k5, k2tog, k2 (11 sts).

Row 28: P to end.

Row 29: K1, k2tog, k1, k3tog, k1, k2tog, k1 (7 sts).

Row 30: P to end; do not cut yarn but change to 2.25mm knitting needles.

Tail fin

Row 31: Incl in each st (14 sts).

Row 32: Incl in each st (28 sts).

Row 33: (K1, p1) 7 times; turn and leave rem sts on a safety pin.

Row 34: (K1, p1) to end.

Rep row 34 five times more, then cast off in rib.

Cut yarn, rejoin to sts on safety pin and work 2nd side of fin to match.

Bikini top

Using two 2.25mm double-pointed needles and C, and leaving a 12in (30cm) tail of yarn, cast on 16 sts using simple cast-on or cable method.

Row 1: (K2tog tbl) 4 times; turn, leaving rem sts on the needle.

Row 2: (P2tog) twice (2 sts).

Row 3: K2tog; fasten off.

Push sts on needle to other end and, with WS facing and using 12in (30cm) tail of yarn, (p2tog) 4 times (4 sts).

Next row: (K2tog) twice (2 sts).

Next row: P2tog; fasten off.

Making up

Stitch back seam of body and head. Run a length of yarn through the stitches at neckline, stuff head and draw up yarn to close opening and shape neck. Stitch seams on each arm piece, pushing yarn ends into sleeves to add a little padding, then stitch tops of sleeves to sides of body.

Stitch back seam of tail, leaving cast-off and cast-on edges in middle of tail open. Fold each side of the fins in half and stitch. Stitch bikini top in place and use tails of yarn to form straps, tying in a bow at centre back.

Using yarn A, make two ears from bullion stitch and oversew the central line of stitches to form a nose. Use black embroidery thread to sew eyes and eyebrows. For the mouth, use yarn D to stitch two small horizontal stitches with a vertical stitch across the centre. (See pages 152–3 for more details about embroidering facial features.)

Use yarn D to stitch hair in satin stitch, taking stitches all along base of hairline to crown of head, then weave long strands through the stitches at the back of the head and a few shorter strands on the top of the head. String beads on to a double thickness of thread and wrap around neck to form a necklace, then stitch a bead to each ear for earrings.

This happy eight-legged sea creature lives on a coral reef with his friends Olwyn and Orlando. They love to sing sea shanties together in three-part harmony.

Octavius octopus

Materials

4-ply knitting yarn in main colour (A) and contrast (B), plus a small amount of black. Coral, rose pink and papaya are used for the coral pieces

2 small buttons

2 x 2.75mm (UK12:US2) double-pointed knitting needles

Pair of 2.25mm (UK13:US1) knitting needles

Tapestry needle

Stitch holder

Size

Octavius's body measures approximately 2¼in (5.5cm) in length.

Tension

See page 142

Pattern note

Octavius is knitted in duck egg with apple-green stripes; Olwyn is dusty pink with banana-yellow stripes and Orlando is peppermint with dusty-pink stripes.

Octopus
(made in one piece)
Tentacles

*Using two 2.75mm double-pointed knitting needles and A, cast on 3 sts.

Row 1: K3; do not turn but slide sts to other end of needle.

Rep row 1 16 times more; cut yarn and transfer to a stitch holder.**

Rep from * to ** seven times more; do not cut yarn after making eighth tentacle.

Body

Row 1: K 3 sts on needle, then k across all sts on holder (24 sts).

Row 2: P to end; do not cut yarn but join in B.

Row 3: Using B, k to end.

Row 4: P to end.

Row 5: Using A, k to end.

Row 6: P to end.

Rep rows 3–6 3 times more then rows 3 and 4 once more.

Row 21: (K2tog) 12 times (12 sts).

Row 22: (P2tog) 6 times.

Cut yarn and thread through rem 6 sts.

Making up

There are lots of yarn ends, so, placing right sides together, use some of them to sew the back seam. Stitch a running stitch around the base of the body and pull up slightly until it fits your finger quite snugly, and fasten off. Then weave in remaining yarn ends: some can be hidden inside the tentacles. Using black yarn, stitch buttons in place for eyes, then embroider eyebrows and a mouth.

Coral
(made in one piece)

These little clusters of coral provide the perfect place for an octopus to perch.

Using 2.75mm knitting needles and coral yarn, cast on 15 sts.

Row 1: Cast off 13 sts, k rem st; turn.

Row 2: K2, turn and cast on 13 sts.

Rep rows 1 and 2 12 times more, then cast off all sts. Do not break yarn but pick up and k 16 sts along edge of work. Cast off all sts and cut yarn, leaving a tail for sewing up.

Making up the coral

Roll up cast-off edge, stitching in place as you go.

Science lab

This cute robot, affectionately known as 'Rick', has bendy arms that allow him to perform all kinds of functions. He will, no doubt, be a key character in all your science-fiction performances.

Rickety robot

Materials

4-ply knitting yarn in pale grey (A) and grey (B)
  plus small amounts of black and white
Pair of 2.75mm (UK12:US2) knitting needles
Pair of 2.25mm (UK13:US1) knitting needles
2 × 2.25mm (UK13:US1) double-pointed knitting needles
Tapestry needle
Polyester toy stuffing
2 × bendy plastic drinking straws

Size

Rick's body measures approximately 2in (5cm) in length.

Tension

See page 142

Body

Using 2.75mm needles and A, cast on 21 sts.

Row 1: K each st tbl.

Row 2: K to end.

Row 3: (K1, p4) 4 times, k1.

Row 4: (P1, k4) 4 times, p1.

Rep rows 3 and 4 nine times more.

Row 23: [K1, (p2tog) twice] 4 times, k1 (13 sts).

Row 24: (P1, k2tog) 4 times, p1 (9 sts).

Row 25: (P2tog) 4 times, p1.

Cut yarn and thread through rem 5 sts.

Head

Using 2.75mm needles and A, cast on 3 sts.

Row 1: Inc1 in each st (6 sts).

Row 2: Inc1 in each st (12 sts).

Row 3: (P1, inc1) 6 times (18 sts).

Row 4: K1, (inc1, k2) 5 times, inc1, k1 (24 sts).

Beg with a p row, work 9 rows in rev stocking stitch.

Row 14: K1, (k2tog, k2) 5 times, k2tog, k1 (18 sts).

Row 15: (P1, p2tog) 6 times (12 sts).

Row 16: (K2tog) 6 times (6 sts).

Row 17: (P2tog) 3 times.

Cut yarn and thread through rem 3 sts.

Arms (make 2)

Using 2.75mm needles and A, cast on 3 sts.

Row 1: K each st tbl.

Row 2: Inc1 knitwise in each st (6 sts).

Beg with a p row, work 19 rows in rev stocking stitch.

Row 22: (K2tog) 3 times (3 sts).

Row 23: P.

Cut yarn and thread through sts.

Nose plate

Using 2.25mm needles and B, cast on 24 sts.

Row 1: K each st tbl.

Cast off knitwise.

Ear plates (make 2)

Using two 2.25mm double-pointed needles and A, cast on 3 sts.

Row 1: K3, do not turn but slide sts to other end of needle.

Rep row 1 ten times more. Cast off.

Making up

Stitch back seam of body. Stitch head seam, stuffing as you go. Stitch head to top of body. Cut a 3in (7.5cm) length from each of the drinking straws, with the articulated section in the centre of each piece. Wrap an arm piece around each one, with purl side facing outwards, and oversew edges together. Attach arms to body, just below head.

Roll up ear pieces and stitch to either side of head. Position one end of the nose plate at centre back of head, with the other end halfway down the front of the head, and stitch in place. For a mouth, stitch a straight line in black yarn. For eyes, stitch centres in satin stitch using black yarn, then outline in backstitch using white.

If you are looking for a leading man to act out your science-fiction fantasies, look no further. He may look mild, in his metal-framed spectacles, but he is extremely cunning and calculating.

Doctor Destiny

Materials

4-ply knitting yarn in white (A), pale peach (B) and coffee (C),
  plus small amounts of raspberry and black
Pair of 2.75mm (UK12:US2) knitting needles
Pair of 2.25mm (UK13:US1) knitting needles
Tapestry needle
Polyester toy filling
4 x tiny white buttons
Two metal bolt rings
Silver embroidery thread

Size

Doctor Destiny's body measures approximately 2½in (6.25cm) in length.

Tension

See page 142

Body and head (made in one piece)

Using 2.75mm needles and A, cast on 20 sts.

Row 1: K each st tbl.

Row 2: P to end.

Row 3: K to end.

Rows 4–6: P to end.

Beg with a k row, work 20 rows in stocking stitch.

Row 27: K4, (k2tog) twice, k4, (k2tog) twice, k4 (16 sts).

Row 28: P to end; cut A and join in B.

Row 29: Using B, k to end.

Row 30: P to end.

Row 31: K6, (inc1 in next st) 4 times, k6 (20 sts).

Beg with a p row, work 9 rows in stocking stitch.

Row 41: (K2tog) to end; cut yarn and thread through rem 10 sts.

Lab coat

Using 2.75mm needles and A, cast on 24 sts.

Row 1: K each st tbl.

Rows 2–3: K to end.

Beg with a p row, work 11 rows in stocking stitch.

Row 15: K5, (k2tog) twice, k6, (k2tog) twice, k5 (20 sts).

Row 16: P to end.

Row 17: K4, (k2tog) twice, k4, (k2tog) twice, k4 (16 sts).

Row 18: P to end.

Cut yarn and thread through all sts.

Collar

Using 2.75mm needles and A, cast on 18 sts.

Row 1: K each st tbl.

Row 2: P to end.

Row 3: K to end.

Cast off knitwise.

Hands and arms (make 2)

Using 2.25mm needles and B, cast on 4 sts.

Row 1: P to end.

Row 2: Inc1 knitwise in each st (8 sts).

Row 3: P to end.

Row 4: K to end

Row 5: P to end.

Row 6: K to end; cut B and join in A.

Row 7: (WS): P to end.

Row 8: P to end.

Beg with a p row, work 13 rows in stocking stitch.

Cast off.

Making up

At base of body, fold first few rows to wrong side along purl ridge and stitch in place to create a hem. Stitch back seam of body and head. Run a length of yarn through the stitches at neckline, stuff head and draw up yarn to close opening and shape neck.

Wrap lab coat around body, placing the two side edges at centre front and draw up the tail of yarn to gather the top to fit. Stitch the edges together from the top to about ½in (1cm) from cast-on edge and stitch the four buttons, evenly spaced, on top of this join. Wrap collar around neck, with ends meeting at the front, and stitch to neckline.

Stitch arm seams, stuffing with any remaining yarn ends, then stitch to top of lab coat at shoulders. Using yarn B, make ears from bullion stitch and oversew the central line of stitches in satin stitch to form a nose. Use yarn C to embroider eyebrows, and raspberry yarn to embroidery a mouth in a single short straight stitch.

Embroider the eyes using black yarn. Thread needle with metallic thread and use it to join together small rings on each bolt ring. Place this join at the bridge of the nose, then stitch side pieces to join the sides of the rings to the tops of the ears.

Create the hair with satin stitch, using yarn C and making vertical stitches radiating from crown to nape of neck and along hairline to tops of ears, then make a small bundle of yarn and stitch it to the top of the head and trim the ends to create a short, spiky effect.

Here's Lucy. Is she a lab technician? A nurse?
Or could she perhaps be the true genius behind Doctor
Destiny's dastardly scientific inventions and experiments?

Lucy lab assistant

Materials

4-ply knitting yarn in white (A) and pale peach (B),
   plus small amounts of geranium red, plum and black
Pair of 2.75mm (UK12:US2) knitting needles
4 × 2.25mm (UK13:US1) double-pointed knitting needles
Pair of 2.25mm (UK13:US1) knitting needles
Safety pin
Tapestry needle
Polyester toy stuffing

Size

Lucy's body measures approximately 2½in (6.25cm) in length.

Tension

See page 142

Body and head (made in one piece)

Using 2.75mm needles and A, cast on 20 sts.

Row 1: K each st tbl.

Row 2: P to end.

Row 3: K to end.

Rows 4–6: P to end.

Beg with a k row, work 20 rows in stocking stitch.

Row 27: K1, (k2tog, k2) 4 times, k2tog, k1 (15 sts).

Row 28: P to end.

Row 29: K1, k2tog, k2, k2tog, k1, k2tog, k2, k2tog, k1 (11 sts).

Row 30: P to end; cut yarn and join in B.

Row 31: K to end.

Row 32: P to end.

Row 33: K3, inc1, k1, inc2 (by knitting into front, back and front of next st), k1, inc1, k3 (15 sts).

Row 34: P to end.

Row 35: K5, inc2, k1, inc1, k1, inc2, k5 (20 sts).

Beg with a p row, work 9 rows in stocking stitch.

Row 45: (K2tog) 10 times (10 sts).

Row 46: P to end.

Row 47: (K2tog) 5 times.

Cut yarn and thread through rem 5 sts.

Hands and arms (make 2)

Using 2.75mm needles and B, cast on 4 sts.

Row 1: P to end.

Row 2: Inc1 knitwise in each st (8 sts).

Row 3: P to end.

Row 4: K to end

Row 5: P to end; cut B and join in A.

Rows 6–8: Using A, k to end.

Beg with a p row, work 9 rows in stocking stitch. Cast off.

Apron

Using 2.75mm needles and A, cast on 12 sts.

Row 1: K each st tbl.

Knit 10 rows.

Row 12: Cast on 6 sts, k to end (18 sts).

Row 13: Cast on 6 sts, k to end (24 sts).

Row 14: Cast off 8 sts, k to end (16 sts).

Row 15: Cast off 8 sts, k to end (8 sts).

Knit 5 rows.

Row 21: K2, turn and leave rem sts on a safety pin.

Strap

Knit 16 rows. Cast off.

Rejoin yarn to st on safety pin, cast off 4 sts and complete 2nd strap to match first.

Hat

Using 2.25mm needles and A, cast on 25 sts.

Row 1: K each st tbl.

Row 2: P to end.

Row 3: K to end.

Rows 4–6: P to end.

Row 7: (K3, k2tog) 5 times (20 sts).

Row 8: (P2, p2tog) 5 times (15 sts).

Row 9: (K1, k2tog) 5 times (10 sts).

Row 10: (P2tog) 5 times.

Cut yarn and thread through rem 5 sts.

Making up

At base of body, fold first few rows to wrong side along purl ridge and stitch in place to create a hem. Stitch back seam of body and head. Run a length of yarn through the stitches at neckline, stuff head and draw up yarn to close opening and shape neck.

Stitch arm seams, stuffing ends of yarn inside them to pad them out slightly, and attach to top of body at shoulders. Wrap apron across front of body, join waist straps together at centre back. Cross shoulder straps at the back and stitch ends to waistline.

Use yarn B to embroider a nose in satin stitch and ears in bullion stitch. Use a little red yarn to embroider a wide mouth, using a single straight stitch held in place in the middle by a small couching stitch, pulling the centre down to create a smile. Embroider beady eyes using black yarn. (See pages 152–3 for more details about embroidering facial features.)

Make a bundle of plum-coloured yarn and stitch to top of head, then stitch in place all round circumference of head, about ½in (1cm) above ears. Embroider a small red cross in the centre front of the hat. Join the seam on the hat and place the hat on top of the head, making sure that the strands of hair emerging from its lower edge are evenly distributed. Stitch the hat firmly in place and trim the ends of the hair.

Who knows where this little creature comes from? Let's call him 'Arnie' until we discover more about him. If he is to take part in your puppet show, you'll have to make up a strange language for him to speak.

Arnie alien

Materials

4-ply knitting yarn in apple green (A) and peppermint (B), plus small amounts of crimson and black

4 x 2.75mm (UK12:US2) double-pointed knitting needles

Pair of 2.25mm (UK13:US1) knitting needles

Tapestry needle

Polyester toy stuffing

Size

Arnie's body measures approximately 2½in (6.25cm) in length.

Tension

See page 142

Head and body
(in one piece, worked
from top down)

Using set of four 2.75mm double-pointed needles and A, cast on 3 sts and divide equally over three needles.

Round 1: K to end.

Round 2: Incl knitwise in each st (6 sts).

Round 3: Incl in each st (12 sts).

Round 4: (K1, incl) 6 times (18 sts).

Round 5: (K2, incl) 6 times (24 sts). Knit 10 rounds.

Round 16: (K2, k2tog) 6 times (18 sts).

Round 17: (K1, k2tog) 6 times (12 sts).

Round 18: (K2tog) 6 times (6 sts).

Round 19: (K2tog) 3 times (3 sts).

Round 20: Incl in each st (6 sts).

Round 21: Incl in each st (12 sts).

Round 22: (K1, incl) 6 times (18 sts). Knit 24 rounds; cut yarn A and join in B.

Round 47: Incl in each st (36 sts).

Cast-off round: *Cast on 1 st, cast off 2 sts, pass st from right-hand needle to left-hand needle, rep from * until all sts have been cast off; fasten off.

Ears (make 2)

Using 2.25mm needles and B, cast on 3 sts.

Row 1: K each st tbl.

Row 2: P to end.

Row 3: K1, incl, k1 (5 sts).

Row 4: P to end.

Row 5: K1, incl, k1, incl, k1 (7 sts).

Row 6: P to end.

Row 7: K1, incl, k3, incl, k1 (9 sts).

Row 8: K to end.

Cast off knitwise.

Arms (make 2)

Using two 2.75mm double-pointed needles and B, cast on 3 sts.

Row 1: Incl in each st (6 sts).

Row 2: P to end.

Row 3: (K1, incl) 3 times (9 sts).

Row 4: P to end.

Row 5: (K1, k2tog) 3 times (6 sts).

Row 6: P to end.

Row 7: (K1, k2tog) twice (4 sts); do not turn but, with RS facing, *slide sts to other end of needle and k4, rep from * 11 times more. Cast off.

Making up

Stuff head and stitch a few small stitches through neck. Weave in yarn ends on cast-on rows of arms, neatening the edges of the hands as you do so. Attach tops of arms to sides of body. Fold each ear in half and stitch side seam, then stitch cast-off edge of each ear to either side of head. With same yarn, create two tufts on top of the head, to represent antennae.

Embroider the face: with black yarn, stitch vertical stitches for each eye and horizontal stitches for each eyebrow. Use red to stitch a small vertical stitch for the nose, then stitch a single straight horizontal stitch to form the mouth, couching it in place using a small vertical stitch in the centre, to form a smile. (See pages 152–3 for more details about embroidering facial features.)

Micky was manufactured by Doctor Destiny from spare parts he found lying around the laboratory. He may look a little strange, but Micky is very quiet, gentle and good-natured – unless you make him angry!

Micky monster

Materials

4-ply knitting yarn in plum (A), white (B), apple green (C) and black (D), plus a small amount of crimson (E)
3 small red buttons
Pair of 2.75mm (UK12:US2) knitting needles
4 x 2.75mm (UK12:US2) double-pointed knitting needles
Pair of 2.25mm (UK13:US1) knitting needles
Safety pin
Tapestry needle
Polyester toy stuffing
Small piece of heavyweight non-fusible interfacing

Size

Micky's body measures approximately 2½in (6.25cm) in length.

Tension

See page 142

Body

Using 2.75mm needles and A, cast on 20 sts.

Row 1: K each st tbl.

Row 2: P to end.

Row 3: K to end.

Rows 4–6: P to end.

Beg with a k row, work 10 rows in stocking stitch; cut A and join in B. Using B, continue in stocking stitch for a further 10 rows.

Row 27: (K3, k2tog) 4 times (16 sts).

Row 28: (P2, p2tog) 4 times (12 sts).

Row 29: (K1, k2tog) 4 times (8 sts).

Row 30: (P2tog) 4 times.

Cut yarn and thread through rem 4 sts.

Head

Using set of four 2.75mm double-pointed knitting needles and C, cast on 3 sts and divide equally over three needles.

Round 1: K to end.

Round 2: Incl in each st (6 sts).

Round 3: Incl in each st (12 sts).

Round 4: (K1, incl) 6 times (18 sts).

Round 5: (K5, incl) 3 times (21 sts).

Knit 12 rounds.

Round 18: (K5, k2tog) 3 times (18 sts).

Round 19: (K1, k2tog) 6 times (12 sts).

Round 20: (K2tog) 6 times.

Cut yarn and thread through rem 6 sts.

Arms (make 2)

Using 2.75mm needles and C, cast on 4 sts.

Row 1: K to end.

Row 2: P to end.

Row 3: Incl in each st (8 sts).

Row 4: P to end.

Row 5: K to end.

Row 6: P to end; cut C and join in B. Using B, knit 5 rows.

Beg with a p row, work 13 rows in stocking stitch. Cast off.

Waistcoat

Using 2.75mm needles and A, cast on 28 sts.

Row 1 (WS): K each st tbl.

Row 2: K to end.

Row 3: K1, p to last st, k1.

Rep rows 2 and 3 three times more.

Right front

Row 1: K4, k2tog; turn and leave rem sts on a safety pin.

Row 2: P5.

Row 3: K3, k2tog.

Cast off purlwise.

Back

Rejoin yarn to sts on safety pin.

Row 1: K16, turn and leave rem 6 sts for left front on safety pin.

Row 2: P to end.

Row 3: K2tog, k12, k2tog.

Row 4: P to end.

Cut yarn and thread through all sts on needle.

Left front

Rejoin yarn to sts on safety pin and work left side to match right side, reversing shaping.

Shirt collar

Using 2.25mm needles and B, cast on 18 sts.

Row 1: K1, incl, k to last 2 sts, incl, k1 (20 sts).

Row 2: P to end.

Row 3: K1, incl, k to last 2 sts, incl, k1 (22 sts).

Row 4: P to end.

Cast off knitwise.

Bow tie

Using 2.25mm needles and E, cast on 10 sts.

Row 1: K each st tbl.

Rows 2–3: K to end.

Cast off knitwise.

Hair

Using 2.75mm needles and D, cast on 3 sts.

Row 1: Incl knitwise in each st (6 sts).

Row 2: Incl knitwise in each st (12 sts).

Row 3: (K1, incl) 6 times (18 sts).

Row 4: K1, (incl, k4) 3 times, incl, k1 (22 sts).

Knit 4 rows.

Row 9: Cast off 4 sts, k to end (18 sts).

Row 10: Cast off 4 sts, k to end (14 sts).

Row 11: Cast off 1 st, k to end.

Rep row 11 five times more.

Knit 2 more rows on rem 8 sts.

Cast off.

Making up

Fold first few rows of body to inside and sew in place. Stitch back seam of body and pull up yarn end on last row to gather up stitches, then stitch to secure. Measure the height of the head and cut a rectangle of interfacing the same width and long enough to be rolled up into a tube to fit inside the head. Insert the tube into the head and then stuff the centre of the tube. Draw up the tail of yarn to close the opening and stitch the head to the body.

Stitch arm seams, stuffing with any remaining yarn ends and attach to top of body at shoulders. Wrap the waistcoat around body, placing the two side edges at centre front and stitch shoulder seams, then stitch tops of front edges together. Stitch one button on top of this join and the other two to the edges of the right front. Wrap collar around neck with ends meeting at centre front. Stitch in place. Bind centre of bow tie with matching yarn then fold each end towards centre and stitch in place.

Using yarn C, make ears from bullion stitch and oversew the central line of stitches to form a nose. Use black embroidery thread to embroider eyes, a mouth and a scar across the forehead.

Stitch seam on hair and fit on to top of head. (See pages 152–3 for more details about embroidering facial features.) Stitch in place, adding a single stitch to the centre front, to accentuate the widow's peak.

When it comes to cleaning, Mrs Moppet is very fastidious.
With her tiny mop and duster, she can get right into every dirty corner,
making sure that the laboratory is spick and span.

Mrs Moppet

Materials

4-ply knitting yarn in Prussian blue (A), beige (B), lilac (C),
  ocean (D) and white (E), plus small amounts of
  geranium red, tangerine and black
Pair of 2.75mm (UK12:US2) knitting needles
Pair of 2.25mm (UK13:US1) knitting needles
Tapestry needle
Polyester toy filling
3in (7.5cm) length of narrow plastic drinking straw
Small round pearl beads

Needle and thread
Red embroidery thread
Fabric scraps: plain yellow and pink gingham check

Size

Mrs Moppet's body measures approximately 2½in
(6.25cm) in length.

Tension

See page 142

Body and head (made in one piece)

Using 2.75mm needles and A, cast on 20 sts.

Row 1: K each st tbl.
Row 2: P to end.
Row 3: K to end.
Row 4: P to end.
Row 5: K1, (yfwd, k2tog) 9 times, k1.
Beg with a p row, work 21 rows in stocking stitch.
Row 27: K4, (k2tog) twice, k4, (k2tog) twice, k4 (16 sts).
Row 28: P to end; cut A and join in B.
Row 29: Using B, k to end.
Row 30: P to end.
Row 31: K6, (incl in next st) 4 times, k6 (20 sts).
Beg with a p row, work 9 rows in stocking stitch.
Row 41: (K2tog) to end; cut yarn and thread through rem 10 sts.

Jumper

Using 2.75mm needles and C, cast on 24 sts.

Row 1: K each st tbl.
Rows 2–5: K to end.
Beg with a p row, work 9 rows in stocking stitch.
Row 15: K5, (k2tog) twice, k6, (k2tog) twice, k5 (20 sts).
Row 16: P to end.
Row 17: K4, (k2tog) twice, k4, (k2tog) twice, k4 (16 sts).
Row 18: P to end.
Cut yarn and thread through rem 16 sts.

Hands and arms (make 2)

Using 2.75mm needles and B, cast on 4 sts.
Row 1: Incl in each st (8 sts).
Beg with a p row, work 5 rows in stocking stitch; cut yarn B and join in C.
Using C, knit 3 rows.
Beg with a p row, work 3 rows in stocking stitch.
Row 13: K1, incl in next st, k4, incl in next st, k1 (10 sts).
Beg with a p row, work 6 rows in stocking stitch.
Cast off purlwise.

Mop

Using 2.25mm needles and D, cast on 28 sts.
Row 1: K each st tbl.
Knit 2 rows. Cast off.

Making up

At base of body, fold first few rows to wrong side along eyelet row and stitch in place to create a picot hem. Stitch back seam of body and head. Run a length of yarn through the stitches at neckline, stuff head and draw up yarn to close opening and shape neck.

Stitch back seam of jumper and slip on to body, pulling up yarn end to fit snugly around neck. Stitch in place. Stitch seams on each arm and sleeve piece, pushing yarn ends into sleeves to add a little padding, then stitch tops of sleeves to sides of jumper.

Use beige yarn to create ears in bullion stitch and a satin-stitch nose. For the mouth, stitch two small straight stitches in red. Use black yarn to embroider eyes. (See pages 152–3 for more details about embroidering facial features.)

Create the hair with satin stitch, using tangerine yarn and making vertical stitches radiating from crown to nape of neck and along hairline to tops of ears. Make a small bundle of tangerine yarn and stitch to front of head to form a little fringe of hair. Cut a triangle from pink gingham (or similar fabric) and wrap around head, tying in a knot at the front, with a few loops of tangerine yarn poking out from under the knot. Secure headscarf firmly to head with matching thread and a few discreet stitches.

String pearls on to a double thickness of sewing thread and wrap around neck, knotting thread ends at the back, to form a necklace. Stitch a single pearl on to each ear for earrings.

Cut a small square of yellow fabric to make a duster and work blanket stitch all around edge, using a single strand of red embroidery thread. Stitch to one of Mrs Moppet's hands. To make up the mop, cut a 3in (7.5cm) length from a narrow plastic drinking straw, wrap the strip of knitting around it and oversew cast-on and cast-off edges together. Make a bundle of white yarn and stitch firmly to one end; trim the yarn ends. Fold Mrs Moppet's hand (the one that is not already holding the duster) over the mop handle and stitch in place using matching yarn.

Naked fingers!

Techniques

How to make your fingers fabulous

Getting started

Yarns

All the projects in this book have been made using four-ply yarn. I prefer to use natural fibres in my knitting projects, particularly pure wool, as it has a natural elasticity – but in some cases I have had to use man-made fibres and various blends in order to source suitable colours. You will need very small quantities of yarn for these little puppets, so before you go shopping for yarns, experiment with any oddments you already have, or shop online for bags containing mixed colours in small amounts.

Needles

Only two different needle sizes have been used throughout this book: 2.75mm (UK12:US2) and 2.25mm (UK13:US1). These are smaller than you might expect in order to produce a firm, close-knit fabric that will hold its shape and not allow any stuffing to poke through. You will need one pair of each size and double-pointed versions for just a few of the component pieces that are knitted in the round. Two double-pointed needles are used to knit i-cords.

Tension guide

Most of the component parts for the puppets in this book are knitted to a similar tension (or gauge) – 15 sts and 20 rows to 2in (5cm), measured over stocking stitch on 2.75mm (UK12:US2) needles, using four-ply yarn. The smaller needles are sometimes used to produce an even firmer result on some of the smaller items such as hats and belts.

To check if your tension matches, work a swatch using four-ply yarn on 2.75mm (UK12:US2) needles and measure it. If you have more than 15 stitches over 2in (5cm), this indicates that you knit more tightly than the stated tension and your puppet is likely to end up smaller than the one in the picture, so you may wish to use a larger needle. If you have fewer stitches, you tend to knit more loosely, so choose a smaller needle. The exact tension is not critical, however, as long as you create a firm fabric that holds its shape and doesn't allow bits of stuffing to poke through.

Stuffing

The puppets' heads are usually stuffed to give a firm result – and so is the Pig's body cavity. Use any commercial brand of toy stuffing for this, or save all the yarn ends you snip off and use these as padding.

Following patterns

Before you embark on any project, make sure you have all the tools and materials you require, then read through the pattern from beginning to end to make sure you understand it. Abbreviations are shown on page 154.

Knitting techniques

Casting on

Simple cast-on

This is the main method used throughout the book; some knitters know it as 'two-needle' or 'chain' cast-on.

1 Make a slip knot and place it on the left-hand needle. *Insert the right-hand needle into the back of the loop, behind the left-hand needle, and wrap the yarn around it.

2 Use the right-hand needle to pull the yarn through the first loop, creating a new stitch.

3 Transfer this stitch to the left-hand needle and repeat from * until you have the required number of stitches.

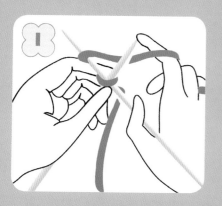

Cable cast-on

This creates a firm edge and can be used as the initial cast-on method or when casting on extra stitches further on in a pattern.

1 Make a slip knot and place it on the left-hand needle. Make one stitch using the simple cast-on method. *For the next stitch, insert the needle between the two stitches on the left-hand needle.

2 Wrap the yarn round the right-hand needle tip and pull through, between the previous two stitches.

3 Transfer the stitch you have made to the left-hand needle and repeat from * until you have the required number of stitches.

Knit stitch

These diagrams show work in progress.

1 To make a knit stitch, insert the tip of the right-hand needle into the next loop, and behind the left-hand needle, and wrap the yarn around it.

2 Use the right-hand needle to pull the yarn through the first loop, creating a new stitch.

3 Keep this new stitch on the right-hand needle and continue along the row.

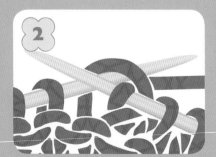

Purl stitch

These diagrams show work in progress.

1 To make a purl stitch, begin with the yarn at the front of the work.

2 Insert the tip of the right-hand needle into the front of the next loop, in front of the left-hand needle, and wrap the yarn around it.

3 Use the right-hand needle to pull the yarn through the first loop, creating a new stitch; keep this new stitch on the right-hand needle and continue along the row.

Other types of stitches

Rows of knit stitches produce a garter-stitch fabric (A); alternating rows of knit and purl stitches produce a stocking-stitch fabric (B) – but when knitting in the round, for stocking stitch you use only knit stitches. Alternating knit and purl stitches along a row produces textured effects, including ribbing (C) and moss stitch (D).

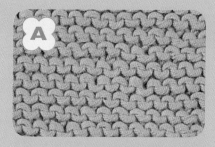

Casting off

This is usually done using knit stitches – but occasionally you will be required to cast off in purl. To avoid confusion, and make it clear which method to use, the pattern instructions will, if necessary, tell you to cast off 'knitwise' or 'purlwise'. Where you are making a ribbed fabric, the instructions will usually tell you to cast off 'in rib' or 'ribwise'.

1 Knit the first two stitches on to the right-hand needle then, using the tip of the left-hand needle, slip the first stitch over the second stitch, leaving just one stitch on the needle.

2 Knit another stitch so that there are two stitches on the right-hand needle, and repeat the process until there is only one stitch left. Cut the yarn and thread the end of the yarn through the remaining stitch to fasten off.

Shaping

The basic finger puppet consists of a tube of knitting that slips over the finger – but to create shoulders, heads and arms, and clothing such as jackets, skirts and hats, you need to shape some of the component parts.

Increasing

Increases are worked by casting on extra stitches at the beginning of a row, or by knitting into an existing stitch twice or three times. Where the pattern states 'inc 1', knit into the front and back of the stitch, thereby creating one extra stitch. Where the pattern states 'inc 2', knit into the front, the back and the front again, creating two extra stitches.

Decreasing

Decreases are worked in a number of different ways.

K2tog: Insert the right-hand needle into the front loops of the next two stitches and knit both stitches together.

K2tog tbl: Insert the right-hand needle into the back loops of the next two stitches and knit both stitches together.

K1, sl, psso: Slip the next stitch on to the right-hand needle, knit the next stitch, then using the tip of the left-hand needle, slip the slipped stitch over the knitted stitch.

P2tog: With the yarn at the front of the work, insert the right-hand needle into the front loops of the next two stitches and purl both stitches together.

P3tog: With the yarn at the front of the work, insert the right-hand needle into the front loops of the next three stitches and purl all three stitches together.

Knitting in the round

Most of the knitted components needed to make up each finger puppet are knitted flat, using two needles, and then stitched together to create three-dimensional shapes. A few of the components, however, are knitted 'in the round' on four needles. Knitting on four needles can be tricky, especially when you are working the first few rows. To cast on, use the two-needle 'simple' method, as it will create a firm, tight edge that is less likely to slip off the needles. For most of the patterns, you will see that the first row (or round) is knitted by inserting the needle into the back loop of each stitch, which also helps to form a firm edge.

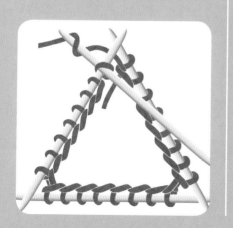

Single-row stripes

This technique is used to make the Ringmaster's trousers. Normally when working in stocking stitch, to work single-row stripes you would have to cut the yarn at the end of each row and rejoin it, creating lots of yarn ends to darn in. This method uses two double-pointed needles removing the need to keep cutting the yarns.

Row 1: Cast on in yarn A; using B, k to end; do not cut B but slide sts to other end of needle and pick up A.

Row 2: Using A, k to end; turn work, pick up B and p to end of row using B.

Row 3: Slide sts to other end of needle, pick up A and p to end of row; turn.

Row 4: Using B, k to end. Continue in this way, working single rows in alternate colours until the desired number of rows have been worked.

Making up

When working on such a small scale, the aim is to be as neat as possible. When joining the sides of two knitted pieces, it is advisable to use one of two methods: mattress stitch or backstitch. When joining two straight edges – usually a cast-on edge to a cast-off edge – oversew the edges for a neat result. This method would be used when wrapping a small strip of knitting around a plastic straw to make the Ringmaster's whip or the Witch's broom, for example. You may also find overstitching the easiest and neatest way to stitch the cast-off row at the top of an arm or sleeve to a body.

Mattress-stitch seam

This method creates an invisible seam.

1 Thread a blunt needle with a long length of matching yarn. With the right side of the work facing, place the two edges together.

2 Starting at the bottom edge of the work, insert the needle under the bar between the first and second stitches on the right-hand side.

3 Insert the needle in the same way on the opposite edge.

4 Repeat, working across from left to right and back again, moving up the seam. Do not pull stitches tight.

5 When you reach the top of the seam, pull the yarn ends until the two sides meet; do not pull too tightly or you will cause the seam to pucker. Fasten off yarn ends securely.

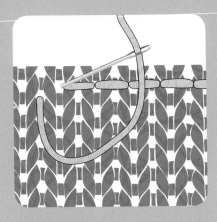

Backstitch seam

This method creates an invisible seam.

1 Thread a blunt needle with a long length of matching yarn. Place the two pieces to be joined on top of one another, right sides together.

2 Working from right to left, one stitch in from selvedge, bring the needle up through both layers then back down through both layers one row to the left.

3 Bring the needle back up through both layers one row to the left, then back down one row to the right, in the same place as before.

4 Repeat, taking the needle two rows to the left each time, and one row back.

Oversewing

Line up the edges to be joined and whipstitch together on the right side of the work.

Gathering (edges)

To gather a cast-on or cast-off edge, thread the tail of yarn into a blunt needle and run the needle through each stitch on that edge, then pull up. If you are closing the hole at the top of a head, for example, run the needle through the stitches a second time and pull up tightly to close the hole, then fasten off the end of the yarn firmly and trim off any excess.

Gathering (shaping)

To gather stitches in the centre of a piece of work – for example, when you are forming a neck between body and head – stitch a running stitch through the stitches of a single row, using matching yarn, then pull up to the required width.

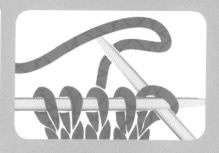

Making an i-cord

The i-cord is a knitted cord that can be made up of two or more stitches. In this book, i-cords are used in various ways – to make arms for the Monkey and the Alien, for example, and to roll up to form the Frog's eyes.

Using two double-pointed needles, cast on the required number of stitches and knit all stitches. Do not turn the work but slide the stitches to the opposite end of the right-hand needle, transfer this needle to the other hand and, taking the yarn firmly across the back of the work, knit the stitches. Repeat the process until the cord is the desired length.

Making a twisted cord

1 Cut lengths of yarn at least four times the length you wish the finished cord to be. Place the strands together and fold in half, then knot all the ends together. Fasten the knotted ends to a stable surface, using a drawing pin to attach them to a solid surface, or a safety pin if this is more appropriate. Loop the centre of the strands over your finger or use a pencil or knitting needle.

2 Keeping the yarn tightly tensioned, twist the strands in one direction; keep doing this until they are tightly twisted into a cord. Still maintaining the tension, grip the centre of the twisted cords between your finger and thumb, then fold in half at this point and let go of the other end, allowing the cord to twist on to itself. Knot the ends and trim.

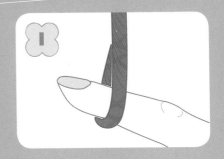

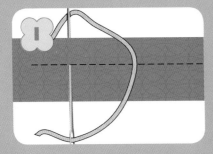

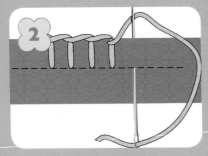

Blanket stitch

This has been used to neaten the edge of the fabric for Mrs Moppet's duster (page 139). You could also use it as a decorative stitch around hems and cuffs. With the edge of the work facing away from you, work from right to left.

1 Bring the needle up at the top edge of the fabric, looping the tail of thread around the needle. Pull the thread taut but not too tight as this will pucker the fabric.

2 The finished stitch should lie flat with the loop of thread forming a bar across the top edge. Repeat step 1 all round the fabric edge.

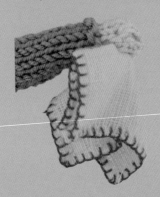

Finishing off

There is more to making a finger puppet than simply knitting the component parts and stitching them together. It is not always easy, when working on such a small scale, to add a lot of detail, but there is scope for creativity. With a few deft stitches, you can alter the angle of a head or the positioning of arms, for example. Even the placement of a hat can make subtle changes to your puppet's demeanour.

Hair

1 Some of the finger puppets in this book have stitched-on hair using satin stitch, while some have more complex hairstyles. Follow the instructions given for each finger puppet or customize the characters by choosing your own hairstyle.

2 To create bushy hair, make a bundle of yarn by wrapping yarn around two or more fingers, then tie firmly around the centre. Stitch the centre of the bundle to the head. If the puppet has a hat or scarf, stitch this in place on top of the hair before trimming the ends of the yarn to create a 'hairstyle'. Experiment with different ways of attaching the bundle until you find a method that suits you. For example, if you tie the bundle of threads quite loosely, you can spread it out across the top and the back of the head and couch the central length of yarn in place from the centre front to the nape of the neck to form a centre parting – ideal if you wish to make a hairstyle that involves plaits or bunches at each side.

3 For wispy hair, separate the strands of thread by running a blunt needle from the top of each strand, where it emerges from the head or the hat brim, to the tip. Trim yarn ends to the desired length.

Facial features

The instructions on these pages will assist you in stitching details such as ears, noses, eyes, mouths and hair – but how you stitch them and in what position will help you to personalize your puppets and create an individual character for each one.

Begin by threading a blunt needle with a single strand of yarn in the colour required. Insert the needle into an inconspicuous point, such as the nape of the neck, and bring it through the work to the point where you wish to add embroidery stitches, so that the end of the yarn is lost inside the stuffing.

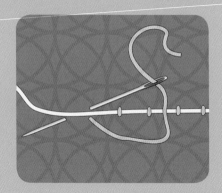

Couching

By couching a straight stitch, you can create a curved line, ideal for an eyebrow or a wide smile. This method can also be used to create a scar – like the one on the Monster's forehead.

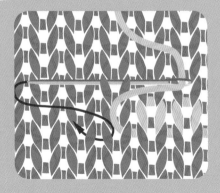

Swiss darning

This is a type of embroidery that replicates the knitted stitch and is sometimes easier than incorporating motifs into the work as you knit. If you look at a row of knitting, you will see that each stitch resembles a 'V'. Thread a blunt needle with yarn and bring it up through the point of the V, then take it behind the two prongs of the V and back down into the point, where you began. This stitch is useful for embroidering a small mouth like Bella ballerina's.

Straight stitch

As the name implies, this is a single straight stitch. In this book, it is used to create simple details such as a small mouth or an eyebrow.

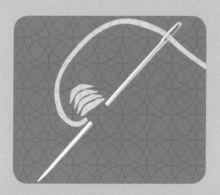

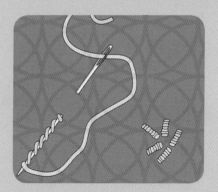

Satin stitch

Use this filling-in stitch for noses or for hairstyles that follow the contours of the head and for the Toadstool on page 83. Bring the needle to one edge of the area you wish to embroider then work straight stitches, close together, to fill in the area. See Dr Destiny's nose as an example.

Detached buttonhole

This stitch is used throughout the book to make ears like Farmer Fred's. Bring the threaded needle through the fabric, emerging at the point where you wish one end of the stitch to be, then take it down through the point where the other end of the stitch will be and back up through the first point. Repeat this process until you have two small loops of yarn. Work buttonhole stitches over and around the two strands that form the loops, then take the needle back down through the end of the stitch and fasten off.

Bullion stitch

You could also use bullion stitch to make ears like Wally wizard's. It is similar in appearance to detached buttonhole.

Fly stitch

This is a simple couched stitch, ideal for a pursed mouth or a little smile like Pixie Pete's.

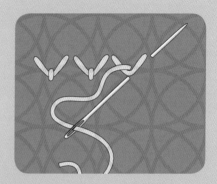

Abbreviations & conversions

Abbreviations

beg	begin(ning)
cont	continue
dec	decrease
k	knit
k2tog	knit 2 together
k3tog	knit 2 together
k2tog tbl	knit 2 together through back loops
LH	left hand
inc	increase
inc1	knit into front and back of same stitch
inc2	knit into front, back and front of stitch
p	purl
psso	pass slipped stitch over
p2tog	purl 2 together
p3tog	purl 3 together
rem	remaining
rep	repeat
RH	right hand
RS	right side
st(s)	stitch(es)
sl	slip
tbl	through back loop(s)
WS	wrong side
yfwd	yarn forward

UK/US yarn weights

UK	US
2-ply	Lace
3-ply	Fingering
4-ply	Sport
Double knitting (DK)	Light worsted
Aran	Fisherman/worsted
Chunky	Bulky
Super chunky	Extra bulky

Knitting needle sizes

UK	Metric	US
14	2mm	0
13	2.25mm	1
12	2.75mm	2
11	3mm	–
10	3.25mm	3
–	3.5mm	4
9	3.75mm	5
8	4mm	6
7	4.5mm	7
6	5mm	8
5	5.5mm	9
4	6mm	10
3	6.5mm	10.5
2	7mm	10.5
1	7.5mm	11
0	8mm	11
00	9mm	13
000	10mm	15

About the author

Artist, writer and designer Susie Johns is simply bursting with creativity. Although she can adapt her skills to a wide range of crafts, she prefers embroidery, knitting, crochet, collage, drawing and watercolour painting – particularly projects that involve recycling and reinventing. Susie has written and illustrated a number of books on a variety of creative subjects as well as having many of her features and interviews published in magazines, such as *Embroidery, Stitches, Let's Knit, Crafts Beautiful, Quick & Crafty, Needlecraft, Beads & Beyond, Family Circle, Practical Gardening, Practical Parenting, Junior* and *Art Attack*. If that's not enough, Susie also takes the time to teach her skills to others at a local community college in London, UK.

Acknowledgements

Thanks to Cygnet, King Cole, Rowan, Coats Patons, Sirdar and Designer Yarns (Debbie Bliss) for supplying the yarns used throughout this book.

A big 'thank you' to Virginia Brehaut for editing and project-managing the book, to Gilda Pacitti and Ali Walper for making it look so attractive, to Anni Howard for patiently checking all the patterns, and to Gerrie Purcell for asking me to do the book in the first place.

Index

To place an order, or to request a catalogue, contact:

GMC Publications Ltd

Castle Place, 166 High Street, Lewes, East Sussex, BN7 1XU United Kingdom

Tel: +44 (0)1273 488005

www.gmcbooks.com